STO AM

ACPL IT Y0-BSM-484

DISCARDED

ARCHITECTURE

Architecture is the only form of art from which we can never escape. A man need never enter an art gallery, may live within bare walls, and reject opera and ballet. He may switch off his radio or television at the first signs of a serious play. But whether he realizes it or not, architecture creates his environment and, to a great extent, determines the kind of life he lives.

This book begins with a discussion of the methods and materials used in construction and then proceeds to the types of buildings that best utilize those methods and materials.

Architecture has perhaps been best defined by German-born architect Ludwig Mies van der Rohe when he said, 'In its simplest form, architecture is rooted in entirely functional considerations, but it can reach up through all degrees of value to the highest sphere of spiritual existence, into the realms of pure art'.

It is the hope that this book may encourage and foster a critical and informed appreciation of the inescapable art of architecture.

G.Z.

A GROSSET ALL-COLOR GUIDE

ARCHITECTURE

BY W. R. DALZELL
Illustrated by Harry Green

GROSSET & DUNLAP
A NATIONAL GENERAL COMPANY
Publishers • New York

1631537

CONTENTS

INTRODUCTION

The four basic methods of construction illustrated below have been used throughout architectural history and are discussed and explained in greater detail later on in this book. Here, very briefly, we see examples of a) post-and-lintel construction, the laying of a horizontal beam across the space between two vertical supports; b) arch construction, covering an open space by placing wedge-shaped units together with their thick ends outward; c) corbel, or cantilever, construction, a projection from the face of a wall, fixed in position to support a weight; and d) truss construction, allowing for the use of a pointed roof.

a

b

c

d

What is remarkable about certain historical buildings, such as the Roman aqueducts, apart from their survival, is not their antiquity, but their modernity. It is true that we tend to admire such a building because of certain romantic or historical associations, or for the rich patina which centuries of weather have given to its surfaces, but the basic architectural beauty of its forms is due to the fact that it represents a contemporary architectural problem solved by the use of the most advanced constructional methods of the time. The beauty of such buildings is an unconscious by-product that arises from an economical and intelligent solution of purely practical problems.

Ideas of what is or what is not beautiful vary from age to age. The splendor of the Gothic cathedrals evoked the contempt and anger of the architects who followed. Like the medieval alchemist searching for the Philosopher's Stone which would transmute base metals into pure gold, the Renaissance architect sought feverishly for mathematical formulae such as the Golden Section which would ensure for his buildings a beauty that was absolute.

The nature of modern architecture is very complex; however, a situation exists which is not unlike the Renaissance/Gothic controversy. The plan of Gothic buildings is organic, often non-symmetrical, and largely determined by the function, the site, the structure of the building and the materials from which it is made. It is sufficiently flexible to enable changes to be made to it without its overall beauty being impaired. The construction is apparent at once—the bones are beautiful and are an integral part of its decoration, which is not normally something applied later to the constructional shell. The building appeals to the emotions, perhaps, rather than to the intellect.

The Renaissance building differs from this in almost every respect. Its plan is like the symmetrical development of a crystal rather than the growth of an organism. The form of the building overrides site, structure and materials, and the nature of the last two is often concealed. The building makes its appeal to the intellect rather than to the emotions. Between these two extremes can be found every shade of compromise. In many ways the buildings of Frank Lloyd Wright are most close to the 'Gothic' and those of Ludwig Mies van der Rohe nearer to those of the classical or Renaissance ideals.

The beauty of such humble buildings as mills and farms is largely the result of the natural material being used correctly for their construction.

Building in Timber

Wherever trees grew, man has used wood from time immemorial to build homes for himself and his dependents, but rarely for buildings of greater architectural importance. This may be due to a certain impermanence, for wood is clearly vulnerable to fire and to attack by insects. Nevertheless, its durability can be demonstrated by the survival of such buildings as the Saxon nave of a church at Greensted in Essex, England and the magnificent *stave* churches of Scandinavia. In Russia and the Baltic countries, where sub-zero temperatures are common, wood is used for both houses and churches for its properties of insulation against the cold, and a great many Russian churches are entirely of wood, even to the onion-shaped domes with which they are decorated.

Wood has always been used in the construction of stone and brick buildings, and the shape of the arches of the Pont du Gard at Nimes, France, is to some extent modified by the

A wooden church in Russia with onion-shaped domes.

The octagonal lantern at Ely, England, one of the most ambitious building projects in wood of the Middle Ages, (begun 1322).

wooden falsework by which they were originally supported. Wooden roofs of great richness and variety appear where the areas were too great to be spanned by a stone vault.

One outstanding example of medieval timberwork still to be seen is the Octagon at Ely Cathedral in England, a mighty wooden lantern made from eight baulks of oak over 60 feet high and each weighing ten tons, built to replace the stone Norman tower after its collapse in 1322. The superb hammerbeam roof at Westminster Hall in London dates from the end of the fourteenth century and covers an area of nearly half an acre. By the middle of the fifteenth century many English parish churches could boast a roof if not as large as that of Westminster, certainly as well constructed and as richly decorated. Only Japan and China have buildings in wood to rival the workmanship of these English churches. The Shoden, the main building of the Ise shrine, exploits the beauty of

The evolution of timber-framed construction, from the crude early
Saxon hut (1), to the splendor of Moreton Old Hall, Cheshire, (4).

the pale yellow cypress wood to the full, but unlike the oak
roofs of medieval England, this shrine is replaced every 20
years, exactly as it was originally built some 1,200 years ago.

All over Europe the humble *cruck* construction of the peas-
ant's hovel gradually developed into a proper timber-framed
house. Vertical timbers gave headroom denied by the sloping
crucks and thus were evolved buildings such as the *hall-houses*
of southern England and of Friesland, with separate rooms for
sleeping and separate accommodation for man and beast.
The in-filling between the timbers was dependent on local
materials. Panels of woven hazel twigs daubed with cow-dung
and clay (*wattle-and-daub*) were inserted between the wooden
uprights, but as these had no great structural strength the timbers had to be close together. With an in-filling of brick and
stone the framework could become more open, and the
exaggerated pattern of such late timber-framed houses as
Moreton Old Hall, in Cheshire, or 'The Feathers' inn at Lud-
low is not due to structural necessity but to an exuberance

of decoration. In Germany, too, where timber was abundant, it was used to build whole streets of splendidly decorative timber-framed houses. Here, too, the upper stories are *jetted* beyond the lower ones, an elementary form of cantilever which provided larger upper rooms and shelter for the foot-passengers below. Many of these houses still survive or have been rebuilt in Nuremberg, Goslar, Brunswick and other German cities. Another widespread traditional method of using timber is to cover the framework with a skin of horizontal wooden planking called *clapboarding* or, in Europe, *weatherboarding*. Houses of this kind are plentiful in Scandinavia.

During the eighteenth century, craftsmen emigrating to America produced versions in wood of buildings of classical form with which they were familiar in Europe. Some of the most beautiful *colonial* buildings of New England and elsewhere, the plantation homes of the South with wide verandahs supported on wooden 'classical' columns, the little meeting

A Japanese shrine built from cypress. One of the superb timber roofs of the English parish churches of the fifteeth century.

Elmwood, home of James Russell Lowell, is built in New England Colonial style.

houses, chapels and churches with wooden belfries and roofs of wooden shingles—all are derived from their stone and brick counterparts in Europe.

Toward the end of the nineteenth century a form of constituted wood, *plywood*, was to make its appearance. This was made possible by the invention in Russia of a water-resistant glue made from casein and blood albumen. The term *plywood* is misleading, and the French word *contreplaque* or the German *Sperrholz* conveys more accurately the arrangement of wooden sandwiches in which the grain of the wood runs at right angles to the layers above and below to produce an immensely strong form of wood. The *laminated* woods, which are a development of plywood, are vastly superior in most ways to the natural woods from which they are made. More recently plastics have been bonded with laminated woods to produce boards which do not deteriorate nor are attacked by insects, and which afford great insulating protection against heat and sound.

A remarkable form of timber roof invented by a German named Zollinger appeared during the 1920's. This consisted of a number of short lengths of timber, known as *lamellas,* locked together to form a roof capable of spanning very large areas without any support from below. In St. Louis, Missouri, an area of 165 feet × 363 feet was successfully covered by a lamella roof.

One of the greatest architects to use wood both as a decorative and a constructional material is the Finnish architect Alvar Aalto. He was one of the first men to realize that in laminated or reconstructed wood was a new material of great strength, however much it might resemble natural wood. Unfortunately, one of his finest examples of the use of wood, the Viipuri Library, with its remarkable undulating roof, was almost entirely destroyed during World War II.

Frank Lloyd Wright always found inspiration for architectural form in Japan, and buildings such as the Sturges house in California and the drafting room at Taliesin West, Arizona, show how much he owes to this influence in the use of wooden forms. Despite the popularity of other materials for building, wood is still used widely.

A modern 'lamella' roof, capable of spanning huge areas without support from the floor; St. Louis, Missouri.

The construction of a temple by the ancient Egyptians, who hauled their stones over huge distances.

Building in Stone

Unlike synthetic manufactured materials with constant compositions and consistent behavior, stone is a natural substance with a great many unpredictable qualities which craftsmen have always had to learn by experience. Some stones are immensely strong, constructionally—granite is three times as strong as sandstone and about ten times as strong as limestone—while others, with great surface beauty, can only be cut into sheets to form a kind of veneer.

In Peru, at Machu Picchu, the Incas erected monumental strongholds of stone reserved for the king, the priesthood and a nunnery, while in the Indus valley, at Ajanta, temples were carved out of the living rock. In Cambodia, Angkor Wat's mighty stone shrines, a complex of temple and mausoleum nearly 2½ miles in circumference, assume the form of a complicated series of pyramids.

Builders of the ancient Egyptian temples hauled their precious stones over huge distances, using it to translate their reed-bundle columns into a more permanent form. The stone columns retain the decorative patterns of the papyrus and lotus stems of their prototypes.

In Greece, stone replaced wood, and the stone temples retain vestiges of the earlier material. The space between one column and another is determined by the distances which a marble block can span with safety. The appearance of Greek architecture today is somewhat deceptive, for originally much of the marble surface was covered with paint. Unlike the Egyptians, who set their vast man-made mountains of limestone sheathed in granite in the empty desert, the Greeks selected the sites for their buildings with great sensitivity. Their theaters are formed from the stone of a curving hillside and were cut largely from the living rock. Thus they achieved a complete harmony between the manufactured building and the natural material from which it was made.

The Romans, on the other hand, made the sites fit their buildings. No suitable hillside for a great amphitheatre was to be found in Rome so they made their own—the Colosseum. They used lava for the foundations, tufa and brick for

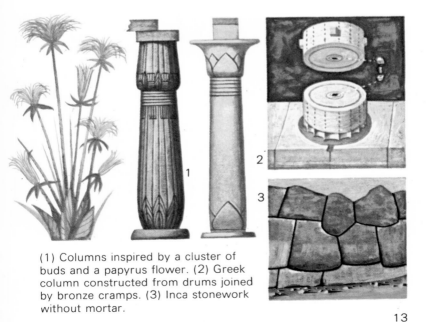

(1) Columns inspired by a cluster of buds and a papyrus flower. (2) Greek column constructed from drums joined by bronze cramps. (3) Inca stonework without mortar.

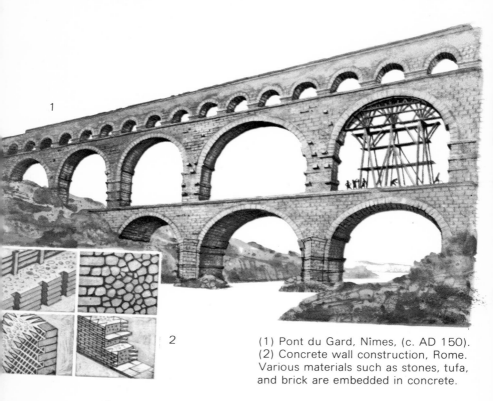

1

2

(1) Pont du Gard, Nîmes, (c. AD 150).
(2) Concrete wall construction, Rome.
Various materials such as stones, tufa,
and brick are embedded in concrete.

the supporting walls and porous pumice stone to lighten the
weight of the vaults, encasing the façade in travertine and
using blocks of marble for the columns and seats. In other
buildings they not only used the post-and-lintel construction
of the earlier civilizations but added a much more complex
one of their own—the arch, which they used with consummate skill. This, together with their invention of concrete,
enabled them to erect viaducts, aqueducts and bridges.

The construction of the arch, however, depended on a pre-
liminary framework of wood known as *falsework,* and the
ledges by which this falsework was supported are still visible
on the Pont du Gard. From the construction of an arch it was
a logical step to build a tunnel, a *barrel vault,* and such was
the skill of the Roman stonemasons that they soon evolved
cross vaults capable of roofing the huge spaces required for

1   (1) Alhambra, Spain. (1309–54).
     (2) Eastern influence in a
2   pierced marble screen, Ravenna.

their palaces and baths. Like some modern architects, they preferred to clad their buildings with sheets of marble, adding false stone columns and moldings to enrich the cheaper material. They used mosaics of stone and pottery as decoration for walls and floors, or fastened sheets of semi-precious stones, such as porphyry and jasper, to the walls.

In the Middle East we find more elaborate forms of arch construction—the horseshoe arch, one with a double curve known as an *ogival* arch, and a complex arch with a multiplicity of arcs known as a *cusped* arch. The sharp tight grain of marble enabled them to drill and to fret thin sheets into screens of great intricacy and beauty—a form of decoration which has been a feature of all Islamic architecture. Muslim influence can be seen in the Romanesque architecture of Sicily and southern Italy, but elsewhere Romanesque architecture is exactly as its name implies. The forms which eventually emerged, however, were only reminiscent of Roman architecture rather than a re-creation of it. There is a great gulf between a real Roman Corinthian capital, for example, and the version produced by a Romanesque carver.

15

The massive quality of Romanesque building was partly lack of experience in working in stone and partly the urgent need for defense. The walls were strengthened at intervals with shallow buttresses, not unlike the Roman pilasters, and were increased in thickness near the base by a form of stone ramp—a device known as *battering* intended to make mining more difficult. The round columns and thick walls were sometimes of solid masonry or of rubble, encased in stone. Windows were tiny, set in the thickness of the walls, which might be as much as 15 or 20 feet thick.

This massiveness of structure is characteristic of all buildings of this period. During the eleventh century, however, two remarkable inventions in the use of stone construction were to revolutionize architecture. The weakness of the Roman cross vault had always been the sharp edge or *groin* which resulted from the intersection of the surfaces. To overcome this weakness Romanesque builders began to build ribs of gently wedge-shaped stones along the edges, filling in the spaces with a web of flat tile-like pieces. They then realized that the ribs were themselves sufficient structure for the vault and that the infilling took a subordinate role. Once the keystone, or *boss*, was in position the whole vault be-

The building of a cathedral.

came an interlocked framework which, as the weight of the building above increased, tended to act as a channel along which the thrust was conveyed to the thick wall, which had to be sufficiently heavy to resist it.

The evolution of the ribbed vault transformed Romanesque buildings, but an even more remarkable discovery was yet to come. While vaulting was confined to a semicircular shape, the various parts of the building had to be the same

The Romanesque arches of the crypt at Canterbury Cathedral, England (2). Compare this semi-circular construction with the later Gothic vaults, with pointed arches, Durham Cathedral, England (1).

width, for the intersection of a 12-foot vaulted passage with another 20 feet wide produced a disparity in the height of the roof which could only be overcome by the ugly and awkward expedient of raising the springing line of the narrower passage on 'stilts'. Almost simultaneously at Durham and in Normandy the Romanesque builders solved these problems by using a pointed vault instead of the traditional semicircular one, and in doing so paved the way for their Gothic successors to exploit the new method of construction so brilliantly. The first effect of the use of a pointed vault was a much greater flexibility of plan. Aisles, cloisters and naves could now be any width required, and yet a roof level maintained by the acuteness or obtuseness of the arches.

During the twelfth century it was realized that, since the thrust of the vault was concentrated at certain points on the walls, it was there only that the wall needed to be so thick, and that if *buttresses* were built to receive the thrust, the walls between could be freed for windows and immense economies in stone and labor effected. As architects and masons became more familiar with this new system of thrust, vaults rose higher and higher and became increasingly intricate, while solid buttresses were replaced by great arched girders of stone called *flying buttresses* which span the roof of the aisle, accepting the thrust of the vault and conveying it through tense arches to carefully strengthened upright members and then safely to the ground. Window areas, small at first, gradually became larger and larger.

The same freedom of the ribs of the vaults appears in the intricacy of *bar-tracery* as the supports of the windows were called. These supports formed lovely flowing shapes which, although they were structurally necessary, were manipulated almost as though they were of a soft malleable material instead of being cut from stone. On the continent of Europe churches of the late Gothic period did indeed show an excess of skill, and stone began to be pierced and cut into lace-like patterns foreign to its nature. Such cathedrals as that at Milan show this overwhelming virtuosity in its most marked form, but every country with the exception of England produced

Vaults became more complex during the twelfth, thirteenth and fourteenth centuries, culminating in fan vaulting.

examples of the straining of this beautiful material beyond its proper limits. In England, the final version of Gothic, known as the *Perpendicular* period, flourished at a time when some of the other countries of Europe were beginning to reject Gothic forms in favor of those demanded by the Renaissance. It is a peculiarly English style, with the sinuous curves of the window tracery frozen into a more rigid grid-iron of stone, but with vaults that become more and more intricate, passing from the more simple *lierne* vault to the full splendor of the fan vaults of King's College Chapel, Cambridge, or of the chapel of Henry VII at Westminster Abbey.

Large numbers of parish churches in every part of England testify to the skill and taste of the English builder-architects of the Perpendicular period. It is to be seen in the diapering of local stone with squares of dark-knapped flint and the lofty naves of the great East Anglian churches, in the splendor of the West Country bell towers with fretted stone panels and in the splendid church porches erected at the expense of the wealthy guilds.

On the continent of Europe, architects of the new Renaissance, inspired by the ubiquitous relics of a golden classical age which they sought to recreate, turned again to the post-and-lintel construction, the semicircular arch construction, and the solid opposition of masses, virtually rejecting the balance of thrust and counter-thrust of their predecessors. They looted Roman buildings for their materials, excavating the fallen columns and embodying them into their new buildings; they ransacked Roman literature for a code of rules of proportion which they applied with a rigidity and pendantry quite unlike the freedom with which Roman architects had used them. Forms used by the Romans for pagan worship were adapted for Christian churches, and the triumphal arch appears once again, only to be applied to the façades of such churches as St. Trophime, near Arles. Only in the development of the dome did they use the technical skills of the Gothic architect, developing this classical feature with an imaginative splendor which far surpasses any Roman achievement.

But the rigid classicism of the Renaissance produced an inevitable reaction, and both the Mannerist architects and the Baroque ones who succeeded them took a willful delight in

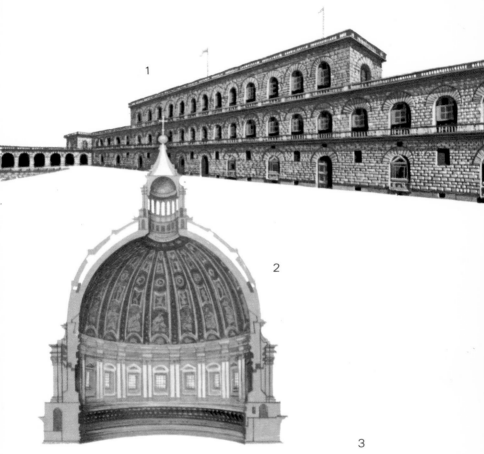

1

2

3

Three Renaissance buildings showing the different treatment and constructional methods used after the Gothic period. 1) Note the heavily 'rusticated' lower courses of the Pitti Palace, Florence, Italy (1435). 2) A section through the dome of St. Peter's, Rome, designed by Michelangelo; incomplete at his death, (1564), it was finished from his own scale model. 3) Vaulted staircase of the Belvedere, Vienna, Austria.

Iron, steel and stone; architecture
of the new Industrial Revolution.

flouting the 'rules' so carefully disinterred by their predecessors. Not only did the plans of buildings become more and more involved, but the wildest liberties were taken with the materials used in constructing and decorating the building. It was as though architects all over Europe were conspiring to perpetrate a huge conjuring trick. Late Gothic carvers might sometimes reduce stone to a froth of lacework, but even they never approached the excesses of technical distortion practiced by the Baroque carvers. A wide variety of stones were integrated with motifs carried out in bronze, in stucco, in plaster and in a range of woods so intimately that it was almost impossible visually to disentangle one from the other. *Trompe l'oeil* painting was practiced with such skill that it is impossible at first to determine whether real columns do actually support real balconies and whether the dome which surmounts the whole interior is itself real, or whether the whole scene is one vast beautiful confidence trick. The natural qualities of stone or metal or wood are subordinated to maintaining a grand illusion, and are made to simulate each other or drapery or human flesh with equal facility. This kind of interior can be seen most clearly in the Pilgrimage Church, Steinhausen, or at another at Ottobeuren, both in Swabia, at the Palace of Bruhl, in the Rhineland, or in Santa Maria della Vittoria, Rome.

This kind of extravagance, while it might be fashionable in the churches and palaces of the great, found little support in more humble buildings throughout Europe. The sort of display suitable to 'Le Roi Soleil' at Versailles would have been far too ostentatious for the ordinary buildings of his citizens or their contemporaries elsewhere.

Where there was a strong local tradition of stone cutting one must expect a certain resistance of the craftsman to change, and such villages as Painswick in England show how slowly and how slightly fashions affected the traditional forms of building in stone evolved over many hundreds of years. Sir Christopher Wren brought vast quantities of Portland stone to London and started a fashion for the combination of stone with brick which is characteristic of English

A typical townscape of heavy industry after the Industrial Revolution.

architecture of the eighteenth century, but perhaps the most delightful effect of English stone building of that time is its unifying influence on such cities as Bath. Here almost the entire city is built from the local stone.

As the Industrial Revolution began to demand the provision of buildings for which there was no precedent—the mills and docks, the bridges and viaducts to carry the new railroads from industry to industry—new uses were found for stone, but it was the engineers and not the architects who were most successful in adapting it to its new role. Such buildings as the Menai Suspension bridge, built by Thomas Telford between 1819 and 1826, show how magnificently stone could be used to solve new engineering problems by a man whose chief concern was functional architecture, not the imitation of historical forms inadequate for contemporary needs.

As iron and steel took over the dominant constructional role, particularly in the New World, buildings could begin to soar, and spaces incapable of being spanned by stone could be bridged. Stone was reduced to acting as an infilling or a cladding to cover the less acceptable bones of the steel or reinforced concrete framework. The development of new and

A 'romantic' exploitation of the qualities of stone in a desert landscape, by Frank Lloyd Wright, at Taliesin West, Arizona, (1938).

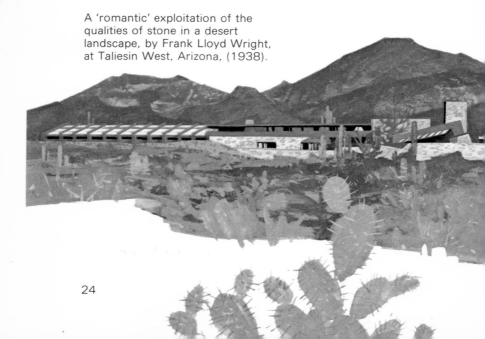

The Fondation Suisse, Paris, by Le Corbusier, (1930–32).

cheaper building materials also caused a decline in the use of stone constructionally. Skilled labor of the kind needed to work stone is expensive and rare, and building in stone is normally a slow and costly business by comparison with casting in concrete. Stone has now, in fact, become a luxury, but its very expensiveness can confer prestige on a building for which it is used. Its rich variety of color and texture, its improvement with weathering and mellowing with time give stone strong advantages over such synthetic materials as concrete, and although stone is now rarely used constructionally, the modern architect is turning more and more to it to give warmth and humanity to his vast buildings. Its ability to 'live with' older buildings (as at Coventry Cathedral) makes it more acceptable in certain circumstances, and it was used with remarkable success by Le Corbusier in the Fondation Suisse, Cité Universitaire, Paris, as a foil to the reinforced concrete construction. Frank Lloyd Wright used stone beautifully and expensively for his own house and studio in the Arizona desert, at Taliesin West, in 1938.

Building in Brick

The early civilizations of western Asia, particularly those in the valleys of the Tigris and Euphrates, found scant supplies of suitable building stone and little timber, but plenty of alluvial clay from which to make both burnt and unburnt brick. Their buildings, therefore, were made from these materials, the vulnerable sun-dried brick being encased in an outer covering of the more durable kiln-baked brick. In Assyria, the brick walls were generally sheathed with thin slabs of carved alabaster or sandstone, while the Babylonians evolved surfaces of glazed tile or brick which enriched the walls with magnificent decorative surfaces as well as offering them greater protection. Unable to find sufficient stone to make columns to support roofs, they evolved an arch and vault construction. Ribbed vaults of brick soon developed the idea of a dome, an architectural feature still dominant in Asia.

That the dimensions of a brick have varied surprisingly little during its long history is due to two factors. A brick must be related to the size of a man's hand, with which it can be grasped and laid, and it must not weigh more than ten pounds when wet, or it becomes unwieldy. It must also be small enough to *fire* evenly in a kiln, without cracking or warping, and it should be about twice as long as it is wide if it is to be bonded properly.

Unfortunately the ancient cities of brick in the Middle East were very largely destroyed by invaders, and the splendid palaces used as quarries for raw materials by their conquerors. More has survived of the ancient Persian Empire, and the tile-faced brick walls of the palaces of Xerxes at Susa have been removed to museums for safety.

Near Baghdad the huge brick arch, over 80 feet wide, which is the most impressive part of the ruins of the Sassanian palace at Ctesiphon, built in A.D. 550, leads to the ruins of a brick-built throne room 160 feet deep with brick walls at least 24 feet thick. These are perhaps some of the most important examples of brick architecture of the Middle East to survive.

The Romans used brick in a variety of ways. Usually brick walls were sheathed in thin sheets of stone or covered with

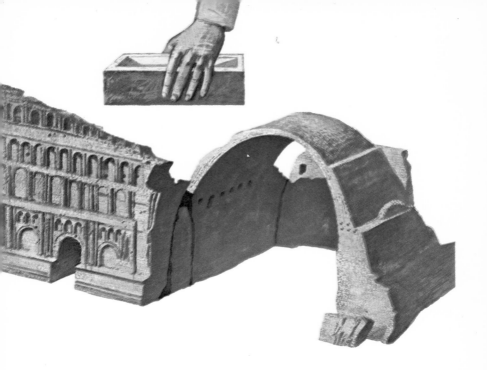

The arch of Ctesiphon, near Baghdad, Iraq, (built c. A.D. 550), is over 112 feet high and 83 feet wide; the earliest arch of this size to survive.

Early brick works, showing the digging of clay, molding and firing of bricks.

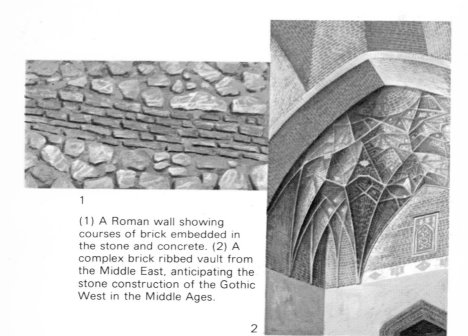

1

(1) A Roman wall showing courses of brick embedded in the stone and concrete. (2) A complex brick ribbed vault from the Middle East, anticipating the stone construction of the Gothic West in the Middle Ages.

2

stucco, a slow-setting lime plaster capable of being modeled or painted. They also used brick as a binding course in stone walls. Many examples of Roman brick were stamped with a wooden mold, giving the name of the estate from which the clay was dug, the name of the brickmaker and occasionally the actual date of manufacture. They normally measure about 18 inches x 12 inches x 3 inches, and are particularly suitable for building arches and vaults.

Although in most examples at Pompeii, Herculaneum and Ostia the covering of stucco has disappeared, the brick walls of the villas and tenement houses are surprisingly sound, and arched doorways, the arches over the ovens and those over the drains are still firm. At Ostia even the temple was built of brick, although faced with marble, and at Herculaneum the poorer houses are brick-framed, the wall panels being a sort of wattle-and-daub. Fragments of burnt brick were mixed in, as part of the aggregate of the famous Roman concrete. Permanent brick ribs, built on a temporary wooden 'falsework' arch, were embedded in concrete to form such remarkable domes as that which covers the Pantheon, in Rome, and to construct the vast vaults of the Roman baths. Brick is also used as part of the complex structure of the Colosseum.

This combination of brick ribs and concrete was adopted from the Romans by Byzantine builders, but their domes of flat bricks do not appear to have been built with any falsework, and they may have derived their constructional principles for these from the East. Bricks of contrasting colors and textures form part of the elaborate patterning which enlivens the brick Byzantine walls on the outside. The facing bricks are not always laid horizontally, but obliquely to form simple chevron, herringbone or fret patterns. Where the courses are horizontal, they alternate with bands of stone or form part of the decorative arches. Inside the building, the raw brick was invariably covered with marble, with mosaic or with some form of painted stucco.

So effective and widespread was the destruction of the Roman civilization by the barbarian hordes in the fifth cen-

The Byzantine method of dome construction, using brick.

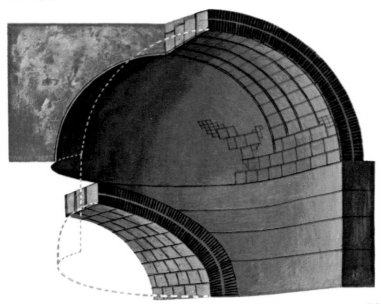

Intricate brick construction of chimney stacks at Hampton Court Palace, England, built during the Tudor period.

tury, that the very crafts of brickmaking and of building in brick died with the men who had practiced them.

Slowly and painfully, civilization re-emerged in Europe, and men again began to build in brick, mainly in the Low Countries and in those parts of Germany ill-equipped with timber and with building stone. Early brick buildings in England were probably built with bricks brought back in ballast by ships exporting wool and cloth to Flanders. The oldest surviving brick dwelling in England is Little Wenham Hall, in Suffolk, built between 1260 and 1280, but it is not certain whether the brick in this instance was made in England or whether it was imported from Flanders.

Flemish refugees who settled in East Anglia were largely responsible for the growth of brick buildings in the four-

teenth and fifteenth centuries, and we find their influence in
the *Flemish bond* by which bricks are still laid and in the
typical gable ends of many Tudor houses. Very few brick
churches are to be found in England, but some magnificent
ones were built in Holland, Belgium and Germany. In England
probably the most impressive house of brick is Hampton
Court, built early in the sixteenth century, and incorporating
Italian terracotta decoration, but its chief glory is the array of
splendidly cut and molded chimney stacks which form such
an impressive addition to its roofline.

Most builders of this period enriched brick wall surfaces by
inserting geometric patterns of differently colored brick.
The rich alluvial clays of the Lombardy plain provided the
brick for some of the most decorative buildings of the Italian
Gothic and Renaissance periods, such as the Ospedale Mag-
giore, in Milan, and the Palazzo Sauli, in Genoa, the latter
built mostly of brick covered with stucco in 1555.

The use of brick in Spain was confined largely to the area around Toledo, where raw materials were more readily available. Moorish overlords were familiar with the brick-building techniques of the Middle East, and their influence lingered long after the expulsion of the Moors from Spain at the end of the fifteenth century.

In England and the Low Countries it became a matter of adapting Renaissance details originally designed in stone so that they could be more suitably carried out in brick. Often a compromise was achieved by adding stone porticos, doorways and pilasters to a brick structure, but classical details were also often cut in brick (*gauged* brickwork) and the mortar joints used to emphasize the nature of the brick surfaces. A brick axe was used to cut the details on such beautiful buildings of the time as the Orangery in Kensington Gardens, London, and gently modeled niches were made by rubbing the brick with a piece of sharp Yorkshire millstone grit.

Building-brick in England and the Low Countries during the seventeenth and eighteenth centuries reached a standard unsurpassed in the history of architecture. It permeated the whole of the architecture of northern Europe, from the delightful almshouses in Haarlem (now the Frans Hals Museum), the 'Queen Anne' vicarages which enrich so many English parishes, to royal palaces such as the Mauritshuis in The Hague, and Hampton Court and Kensington Palace in England. Christopher Wren used brick with consummate sensitivity and skill for some of his London churches after the Great Fire of 1666, and the tradition was carried on by such architects as the Adam brothers until the end of the eighteenth century. Covering his brick structure with a creamy stucco, John Nash built the terraces which encircle Regent's Park in London, and in doing so created one of the finest townscapes in Europe.

At first the clay was dug locally, but the opening of the Bridgewater Canal in 1761 enabled a series of waterways to be created by which bricks could be transported all over the country for the new buildings demanded by the Industrial Revolution. The reeking kilns of the Black Country, the mill towns of the North, the new viaducts, railroad bridges and tunnels of the new railroads linking the industries to the new warehouses and the harbors all demanded the use of brick.

A severe brick house of the Queen Anne period. Formally designed, it contains such impeccable craftsmanship as that shown in the 'gauged' (carved) and rubbed brick capital, and in other classical details.

St. Katherine's Dock, London. Brick was used extensively for the buildings of the new Industrial Revolution. (Thomas Telford, 1824-28).

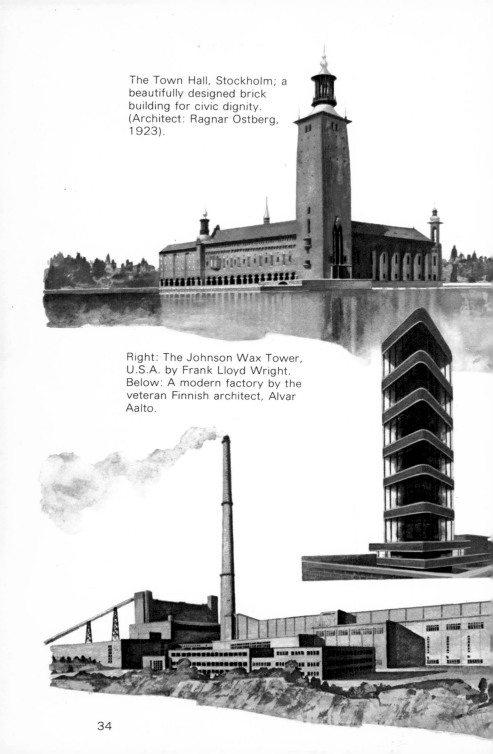

The Town Hall, Stockholm; a
beautifully designed brick
building for civic dignity.
(Architect: Ragnar Ostberg,
1923).

Right: The Johnson Wax Tower,
U.S.A. by Frank Lloyd Wright.
Below: A modern factory by the
veteran Finnish architect, Alvar
Aalto.

These all laid the foundations for the great brickmaking industry of England which serves the builders of the twentieth century.

It was clear that as the evolution of steel-framed and reinforced concrete construction continued, they would replace the more traditional uses of stone and brick. The speed with which buildings could be constructed from prefabricated parts in the factory was far in excess of that with which brick buildings could be erected. It seemed that brick would henceforth play a very subsidiary part in building construction, a kind of in-filling to other constructional methods or as a cosmetic to relieve the monotony of reinforced concrete.

Brick has, however, considerable advantages. The wide variety of textures and colors not only makes it an excellent foil to other materials. It also enables it to be assimilated far more easily into landscapes or townscapes where more aggressively modern materials would jar badly. Unlike them, it improves with weathering, and its properties of insulation and of durability are remarkable. The very smallness of a brick has its own advantages. It can be used more readily on buildings with an intricate plan or undulating curves, and it needs no heavy equipment which might be difficult to maneuver on a limited site. Above all, its small scale and domestic associations make it peculiarly suitable for houses. Finally, in certain areas at least, craftsmen and architects have been working with brick for hundreds of years.

Some of the best modern buildings in brick are in the Low Countries, in Germany and in England. They include many buildings by Willem Dudok, the municipal architect of Hilversum, and those by Jacobus Oud, a creative architect who belonged to a group of artists and architects called *De Stijl*, which exerted much influence on European architecture in the later 1920's. A late work by the veteran German architect Peter Behrens, the Hoechst Dyeworks offices, is typical of the romantic appreciation of the surface quality of brick. In England brick has been used with great success at the Engineering Building, Leicester University, by James Gowan and James Stirling. Its unique qualities are exploited by Alvar Aalto at his Civic Center in Saynatsalo, in Finland, and as a brilliant in-filling by Frank Lloyd Wright in the famous Johnson Wax Tower in the United States.

Building in Concrete and Other Materials

The discovery that a mixture of a volcanic earth called *pozzolana* and lime could make the most powerful cement yet known was to have far-reaching consequences not only in Roman architecture but in the development of architecture in the western world. The famous Roman concrete consisted of this pozzolana cement mixed with an aggregate of broken tile and burnt brick, tufa and some other suitable stones poured into planked shuttering (like modern concrete) with alternate layers of large and small stones. It produced a concrete so durable that, even after 2,000 years, fragments of an aqueduct built from it defied the efforts of modern engineers to remove it when they needed airfields in the area during World War II.

The advantages of such a synthetic stone to a nation whose armies were establishing colonial cities in every corner of the known world were obvious. With almost unlimited resources of unskilled labor, a handful of technicians could erect Roman cities in countries where there was neither suitable building stone nor craftsmen to work it. A raw concrete surface seems to have been as unacceptable to the Roman architect as it is to some of his modern successors, and it was usually sheathed with thin sheets of marble or some other decorative stone, or clad in brick.

The Roman builders found concrete particularly suitable for the construction of domes and vaulted roofs. The dome of the Pantheon, in Rome, is over 140 feet in diameter—a great concrete shell with brick ribs which rests on concrete walls 20 feet thick. Huge areas of the Baths of Caracalla, also in Rome, are vaulted with concrete.

Although the use of concrete continued after the fall of Rome in the eastern half of the Empire, it seems to have lapsed considerably elsewhere. Gothic builders used it for foundations, more sparingly as an additional means of construction to basically stone buildings, and for fortifications. A limited use of concrete was made by their Renaissance successors.

More modern developments in the use of concrete, however, date from the erection of the third Eddystone lighthouse, built off the English coast by John Smeaton in the 1750's to replace a timber construction destroyed by fire. He used con-

The Baths of Diocletian, Rome,
(A.D. 284). Concrete and brick
sheathed in marble or stucco.

Notre Dame de France, London. Iron vaulting and rib construction. St. Peter's, Rome. Early use of iron reinforcement, by encircling chains in dome construction.

crete to assist in the interlocking of the stones from which his lighthouse was composed, a device which lasted until the end of the nineteenth century when the structure was transferred to Plymouth Hoe. In 1796, James Parker discovered natural materials on the Isle of Sheppey for making cement which was not only fast-setting but suitable for use under water for harbor installations. The cement he called 'Roman Cement', a commercial 'gimmick' to attract customers. Another rival, however, Joseph Aspkin, discovered rich sources of material for an artificial cement at Northfleet, in Kent, and called his cement 'Portland Cement' implying its resemblance to the famous stone. He and his son opened works at Northfleet, laying the foundation of a great industry.

Before dealing with the reinforcing of concrete with iron and steel, the next major step in its use, we must turn our attention to the architectural use of iron itself. It had been used sparingly as a structural material during the Middle Ages. Indeed, iron tie-rods inserted in the vaults of Westminster Abbey to compensate for the slow setting-time of the medieval mortar are still in position. Renaissance architects such as

Palm House at Kew Gardens, London. Early prefabrication of iron and steel components.

The earliest iron bridge in England, (Coalbrookdale, Shropshire, 1779).

Brunelleschi and Michelangelo had embedded iron bands in the stonework of their great domes to strengthen them, but this and other attempts to combine stone and iron were not very satisfactory, for masonry joints can never be wholly watertight, and the iron, expanding at a different rate from the surrounding stone, tended to open the joints and to allow rust to accumulate. It was the eighteenth-century engineers, such as Abraham Darby in England, who developed iron as an architectural material in its own right. Abraham Darby III, his grandson, built the first iron bridge at Coalbrookdale in 1779 but iron was developed largely in order to find a fireproof material with which to build the mills required by the Industrial Revolution.

One of the first examples of the use of iron in architecture was for the roof of the Théâtre Français in 1786, and when Jacques Soufflot embedded iron bars in mortar for his great church of St. Geneviève (now the Panthéon) in Paris he anticipated the development of reinforced concrete by a hundred years. In England, John Nash used iron structurally at Carlton House Terrace, London, and at the Brighton Pavilion early in the nineteenth century, but the iron pillars at Carlton House Terrace are painted to look like stone, and those at the Pavilion were disguised as palm trees and bamboo! The spire of Rouen Cathedral, begun in 1823, is also of cast iron, but iron was to be used much more frankly by Decimus Burton in his great Palm House at Kew, London, in 1844–48.

The Crystal Palace of 1851 gave great impetus to the prefabrication of iron building units, but this was not designed by an architect, and architects continued to regard this material as unworthy of serious architecture. John Ruskin declared prophetically, 'The time is probably near when a new system of architectural laws will be developed, adapted entirely to metallic contruction', and in France, Louis-Antoine Boileau had already successfully erected in 1854-55, the church of St. Eugène, with cast iron columns and vaults with iron ribs. He followed this with an iron-framed church—Notre Dame de France, near Leicester Square,

2

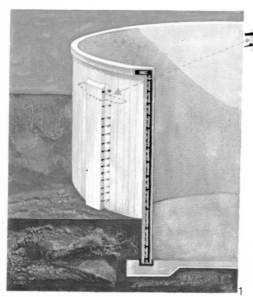

(1) Pre-stressed concrete tank for the British Ministry of Works, showing metal reinforcing embedded in concrete shell. (2) Section of reinforced concrete pilaster, showing metal in position.

Reinforced concrete mushrooms support slab constructions.

London, which he converted from an old circular Georgian building called the Panorama (see page 38). Cast iron was also used for the roof construction of the Houses of Parliament and for the tower housing Big Ben.

The first wholly iron-framed building was a chocolate factory at Noisiel-sur-Marne, in France, and engineers now sought a method by which iron and concrete might be combined so that the weaknesses of one material might be offset by the strength of the other. An experimental concrete boat with a mesh of iron rods embedded in concrete to form the frame led to more serious consideration of this type of structure for architectural purposes, and by 1898 François Hennebique was able to evolve a complete method using concrete with steel instead of iron. E. L. Ransom, an Englishman, built the first concrete-framed building in America, at Greenburg, Pennsylvania, in 1902.

In the meantime, improvements in the quality and manufacture of iron and steel, making them more effective for

Interior of the Centenary Hall,
Breslau. Early use of reinforced
concrete by Max Berg, 1912–
13 (above).

Seagram Building, New York,
designed by Mies van der Rohe.
Cantilevered floors enable walls
to be suspended, the walls no
longer support (right).

architectural use, enabled some American architects to
exploit these materials in unprecedented forms of building.
At Buffalo, Louis Sullivan erected one of the first metal-framed
skyscrapers, the Guaranty Building, in 1894, following with
the Carson, Pirie, Scott and Company building in Chicago in
1899. The disastrous fire which almost destroyed Chicago in
1871 and the terrible earthquake and fires in San Francisco in
1906 undoubtedly made American architects more receptive to
the new architectural materials than their contemporaries in
Europe. Auguste Perret had demonstrated the use of reinforced
concrete by building the first apartment houses in this material
in the Rue Franklin, in Paris, in 1903 (and was to build a
magnificent reinforced concrete church, Notre Dame de
Raincy, in 1932), but it took a long time for European architects to realize that reinforced concrete was an entirely new
medium, and not a cheap way of building in stone.

Beautiful curved shapes of great economy and efficiency
appeared in a succession of bridges from 1905 onward carried
out by Robert Maillart, a Swiss engineer who had been

a pupil of Hennebique. The remarkable potentialities of reinforced concrete for the construction of a dome were exploited for the first time by Max Berg with his Jahrhunderthalle roof at Breslau in 1910–12. Here, an area of nearly 21,000 square feet was covered by a roof weighing only 4,200 tons. The concrete members of which it was composed were left exposed and added greatly to the airy beauty of the building. It is worth comparing the dome of reinforced concrete with that designed in stone by Michelangelo at St. Peter's, Rome. The Michelangelo dome, which weighs 10,000 tons, covers only an area of 5,250 square feet. In 1911, another original young architect, German-born Walter Gropius used a steel frame with an in-filling of sheet glass for the Fagus factory at Alfeld-an-der-Leine and was to develop this combination of glass and steel more fully in his model factory at the great Werkbund Exhibition in Cologne three years later.

World War I was to check the progress of architecture in Europe, although the famous airship hangers at Orly,

Brilliantly designed reinforced concrete bridges span gorges with maximum efficiency and minimum amount of material (Architect: Robert Maillart).

The potentialities of reinforced concrete exploited by Nervi (1) and Maillart (2).

designed in 1916 by Paul Freyssinet, showed that the lessons learned in peacetime could not be entirely forgotten during war. Freyssinet was later to build a number of magnificent bridges in reinforced concrete. Of these, two outstanding examples survive unscathed — one carrying the motorway near Caracas, Venezuela, the other being the Treneberg Bridge in Stockholm, Sweden.

The Deutscher Werkbund was revived after World War I, and a housing exhibition superintended by Mies van der Rohe was staged in 1927 near Stuttgart. A number of young architects participated at his invitation — Walter Gropius and Le Corbusier, both pupils of his own teacher, Peter Behrens (who also took part); J. J. Oud, the Dutch architect; and many others. Mies van der Rohe himself contributed a block of apartment houses. All the houses were required to have flat roofs and were constructed either with steel framework, or with supports of reinforced concrete or steel girders, or both. These enabled the floors to be cantilevered out and allowed walls to be carefully proportioned panels, virtually suspended from the upper floor and roof. The open plans which resulted from this type of construction were to point the way to a new series of spacious architectural forms which even today are considered to be ultra-modern. The lumpiness often associated with reinforced concrete gave way to a more imaginative, airy treatment.

By the 1930's elegant mushroom-shaped supports were evolved by Sir Owen Williams to hold the cantilevered floors of the extensions to Boots Chemical Factory near Nottingham, England, and by Adams, Holden and Pearson, the architects of the new underground railroad station at Arnos Grove, for its central booking hall, in 1932 (see page 41).

In the meantime, architects were experimenting with the remarkable possibilities which this new material offered. It was soon realized by Freyssinet that the weight-bearing properties of concrete could be increased and the weight and size of the members could be reduced if the rods inserted in the concrete shapes could be put in under tension. This method, which he patented in 1928, is called *pre-stressed concrete,* and the structures this produced are able to resist tensile stresses put upon them more effectively. The familiar beam-type

Penguin Pool at the Dudley Zoo in England, by Tecton, (1938).

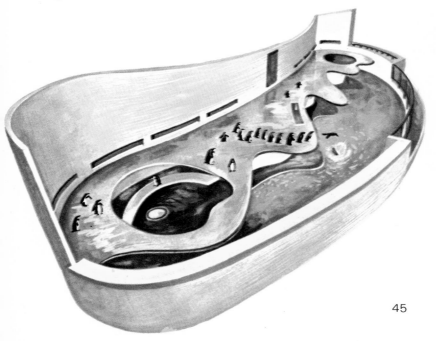

45

structure resists weight put upon it by sheer strength, and this, in turn, often demands excessive bulk of concrete and steel—a disadvantage if large areas have to be roofed.

Two engineers, Walter Bauersfeld and Franz Dischinger, experimented with a different type of structure—a concrete shell. The principle can be best explained by laying a sheet of paper across the gap between two books. It will sag at once if any weight is placed upon it. If, however, the paper is formed into a curve by compressing it gently between the two books so that it forms an arch between them, it at once becomes capable of bearing weight.

Pre-fabricated buildings under construction. Components are manufactured in factories and assembled on the site (below).

The suspended roof of the Arena, Raleigh, North Carolina, built (1952–53) by Nowicki, Deitrick and Severud (right).

The strength of such a shell construction depends on weight being distributed uniformly over its thickness. One of the first practical examples was carried out by Walter Bauersfeld in 1926 in Jena, where he constructed a shell dome over the Planetarium, covering a mesh of steel with a thin skin of concrete. Other modern architects were quick to realize the immense potentialities of this new method of handling concrete. With it Freyssinet made a barrel vault to cover the market hall at Rheims in 1928–29, and six years later the Spanish civil engineer Eduardo Torroja used it in a most original way to produce the great cantilevered roofs for the grand-

stands at the racecourse (Zarzuela Hippodrome) near Madrid.

It was becoming clear that here was a material which, since its steel reinforcement could be bent into complex curves during manufacture, could undertake curvilinear shapes unlike those of any traditional material, and, unsupported by additional columns, could reach out far in excess of the timid cantilevering of wood and stone. Nevertheless, some of the concrete 'post-and-lintel' buildings of the 1930's look depressingly dull, and it was left to such charming and witty exercises in reinforced concrete as the ramp for the Penguin Pool at the Dudley Zoo in England to show what could be done in this way. The ramp was designed by a group of very serious architects called 'Tecton', led by a former pupil of Auguste Perret, a Russian named Lubetkin (see page 45).

In Florence, the brilliant Italian engineer Pier Luigi Nervi designed a much more ambitious building at about the same time, exploiting the curvilinear qualities to be seen, in miniature, at the Penguin Pool. This, the Berta Stadium, opened in

1932, was the prelude to some of the most remarkable reinforced concrete buildings in the world. Nervi began to explore the possibilities of building with a series of carefully designed reinforced concrete units, and the immense floor of his Exhibition Hall in Turin, built in 1948–49, was the culmination of experiments extending over a number of years. He also evolved a system of ferroconcrete molds with which he cast concrete units on the site—enabling him to erect the superb little Palazzetto dello Sport for the Olympic Games of 1958 in less than six months.

Materials other than reinforced concrete can also be used for prefabrication and it is in this field that the plastics, unknown 50 years ago, are rapidly becoming of paramount importance. Their lack of success at first was due to the wide range of synthetic materials embraced by the word *plastics* and the failure of the designers using them to realize that they were all entirely new substances and not merely substitutes for wood or metal. The group possesses many remarkable properties. They are extremely light and their tensile strength to weight ratio compares very favorably with that of many metals. They are resistant to weather, to attack by industrial fumes and to most chemicals, and although they are combustible, most are non-inflammable.

The subordinate role of plastics in providing only components such as guttering and electrical equipment is now being superseded by their use, in conjunction with traditional materials, for constructional purposes. They are particularly suitable for the production of weight-bearing 'sandwich' panels, which consist of strong wear-resistant plastic skins bonded to light low-density cores of other plastic materials with excellent thermal insulating properties. This property of thermal insulation can also be used with traditional brick cavity walls, the spaces being filled with some form of polystyrene foam. Very successful experiments in the production of complete bathrooms and central plumbing units have now made it commercially possible to insert such a 'heart' unit during the construction of a building. The whole complex is produced as part of a single process, with every component an integral part of design.

Some of the most striking examples of the constructional

The new plastic materials are beginning to initiate new architectural forms, as in this geodesic dome construction. A complete kitchen and bathroom unit made from synthetic materials is lifted into position and the house built around it.

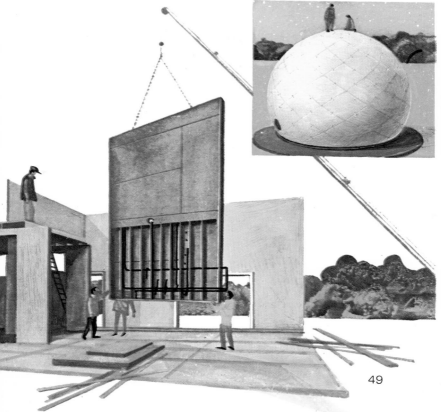

49

An entirely new concept of industrialized housing called 'Habitat' erected experimentally at Expo '67, Montreal, Canada, by Moshe Safdie.

use of plastics have been the *radomes* built to house radar antennae and electronic equipment. Those in the United States and Canada have been as high as 116 feet, with a base diameter of 105 feet and an equatorial diameter of 140 feet; others are in production which will be considerably larger than these. These radomes are constructed from a series of carefully calculated geometric shapes which, when fitted together, form a spherical icosahedron. The panels can be made of expandable polystyrene and polyurethane foam about three inches thick and measuring about 3 feet x 4 feet. They are protected by a skin of glass cloth cemented to the foam with epoxy resin. When properly fitted and the joints protected, such a dome will withstand a wind velocity of up to 250 miles per hour.

Other dome structures have been made from panels of thin sheets of reinforced fiberglas. Indeed, fiberglas is far more familiar as a roofing material than some of the other plastics, and as a constructional material is rapidly becoming as popular in architecture as it has already become in the manufacture of boats, trailers and cars. The methods by which plastic shapes are produced has led to an entirely new appearance to architectural forms embodying plastics. Both as adjuncts to traditional methods and as building materials in their own right, plastics are bound to contribute to the architecture of the future.

With the revolution which has taken place in methods of construction and production of buildings, with new materials being added almost yearly to those used since the beginning of architectural history, and with greater demands for every kind of building to raise living standards all over the world, it is clear that we shall have to be less conservative in our approach and more willing to accept unfamiliar forms of architectural design. It may well be that the project of multiple housing known as 'Habitat', shown at the Expo '67 exhibition in Montreal, Canada in 1967, anticipates the appearance of some of our cities in the future. Each living unit at 'Habitat' has a terrace and garden located on the roof of the unit below. The units were precast in concrete and a crane lowered them into their proper place.

Modern developments. The new shopping
center, Rotterdam, Holland.

A Norman 'motte and bailey' castle, and a section through the keep.

Matsumoto Castle, Japan, founded in the sixteenth centu

Buildings for Defense

In the past, castles and other fortifications were normally classified as 'military engineering' and banished from the architectural scene at once. Today, with architects and engineers far more closely linked than in the past, we are more ready to accept the idea that because a castle had been designed primarily to provide a well-protected home for its occupants, it has a certain clarity of form, a logic of plan, and a unity of material and function which we would regard as essentially architectural. It is the same unconscious beauty which we find in the well-designed shapes of the armor with which the owners of the castles encased their bodies. Once the site of the castle had been decided, the form of the castle would be dictated by the materials with which it was to be built, the many complex services it had to provide for the community within its walls and the functions it had to perform. Although its role was a defensive one, it is worth stressing that in fact it was rarely under siege and that for most of its life it had to provide much more than a sort of corporate suit of armor. It could be expected to act in times of peace as the center of local government and to become periodically a hall of justice and perhaps even a jail.

As a home for a self-supporting community it had to have a supply of good water which could not be interfered with if the castle should be besieged, and it had to have good drainage for sewage. Facilities had to be provided for the production and storage of large quantities of food—a kitchen and bakery, a dairy, a butchery, and a brewery—besides facilities for weaving cloth, for tanning leather, a smithy and all the needs of a medieval community, including a chapel for daily worship. Certain places of work, such as the sawpit and the smithy, could be sited outside the precincts of the castle in peacetime, but when war threatened, the surrounding countryside might well be subjected to a 'scorched-earth policy' to deny supplies to the aggressor, and the whole community, its animals and its possessions be brought within the walls for protection.

It was essential that the castle should be able to combat various forms of attack and that its design should be flexible enough to meet new forms of attack. It had to be able to resist direct assault by night and day, to make undermining difficult, if not impossible, by some form of moat or by making the walls impenetrably thick at ground level. It had to be equipped to deal with attack by fire, to be able to repel engines of war and, finally, it had to meet the growing menace of gunpowder and artillery. Its occupants had to be able to hold out against starvation and thirst, and eventually to abandon their passive role and go over to attack. In Japan, there was an emphasis on archery long after it was obsolete in Europe, and different forms of architecture evolved. This can be seen at such fortresses as Osaka Castle, completed in 1587, and Matsumoto Castle, founded in the sixteenth century, with their sloping, wide stone bases and shuttered wooden galleries (see page 52).

The evolution of the castle in Europe shows how well builders understood the problems involved. When William the Conqueror invaded England he brought with him a number of pre-fabricated strongpoints of timber which were hardly castles, but which, when assembled, acted as temporary forts. These developed into *motte and bailey* castles, a form of castle which, lacking a natural hill, was built on an artificial mound known as a *motte*. The main strongpoint was the rectangular central *keep*, or *donjon*, several stories high and encircled by a curtain wall enclosing a large area known as the *ward*, or *bailey*. The shallow buttresses appearing at intervals on the walls and at the corners are perhaps vestiges of the great balks of timber with which the original strongpoints were strengthened. Local stone would be used if it was suitable, but the keep of the Tower of London, now known as the White Tower, was built from vast quantities of stone imported by William the Conqueror from his native Normandy. The simple motte and bailey plan of a twelfth-century fortress proved to be adequate for the methods of attack at that time, but experience during the Crusades soon produced more sophisticated forms of attack, and the famous Krak des Chevaliers in Syria is a far more highly developed form of castle than the Tower of London. New forms of attack made it necessary to build

A full-scale attack on a castle. Notice how the defenses are designed to anticipate every known form of attack.

A completely fortified town known as a 'bastide' town.

defenses in depth and to enclose the main strongpoint in a series of concentric rings of defense with an outer bailey added to the inner bailey, each defended by a series of high walls with watch towers which were mutually defensive.

High walls made trebuchets and other weapons less effective, but unfortunately they offered a certain amount of cover to miners burrowing at the base of the wall. To counter this, temporary wooden galleries known as *hoardings* were built out on brackets and overhung the base of the wall.

To study the way in which whole towns constituted a completely defensive system it is necessary to go to Siena or Gubbio in Italy, to Avila in Spain, or Carcassonne in France, where a state of war kept the townspeople alerted long after the English had been able to let their city walls crumble and their towns sprawl into the surrounding country. The only time in which the English found it necessary to build new castles was during the reign of Henry VIII when a threat of invasion caused him to have a ring of them built from Hull to Cornwall. These include the castles of Deal and Walmer, equipped to defend themselves against artillery and to make the anchorage off Deal safe from a hostile fleet, and pairs of castles such as Portland and Sandsfoot, Pendennis and La Mawes, which could be linked by iron chains to deny access to the river mouths they guarded.

On the mainland of Europe, however, towns such as Aigues-Mortes, in France, began a pattern of *bastide* towns — that is, towns with turretted towers and battlements which were themselves a complete system of defense — and this continued into the seventeenth century. Towns such as Middelburg and Arnhem in Holland, Mannheim in Germany and St. Rochelle in France show how their medieval fortifications were absorbed by more sophisticated *stellate,* or star-shaped, schemes of defense calculated to defend their cities against artillery. Each point of the star is itself a strongpoint providing covering fire for the others and constituting outer defenses which had to be silenced before the attacker could even begin to deal with the defenses of the actual city itself.

The star-shaped town of the Renaissance organized against artillery.

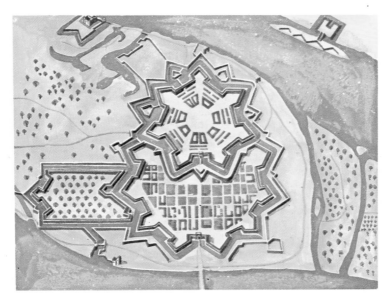

Buildings for Living

For a very long time, the needs for defense took precedence over comfort and convenience, and in the early communities it is impossible to make any clear distinction between buildings for defense and buildings in which to live. This is equally true whether we study the remains of the early cities of the Indus Valley, built in brick about a central citadel, or the mysterious stone fortifications of the ancient city of Zimbabwe in Rhodesia. The palace at Knossos, in Crete, those of the Persian despots at Persepolis and the massive ruins at Mycenae are examples of domestic architecture of a Mediterranean people, living largely in the open air, but clustered for mutual protection about their rulers.

In ancient Egypt, palaces appear to have been designed with the rooms disposed more or less symmetrically about a series of open courts, but the ruins are scanty, and of the baked brick and mud houses of the ordinary men, nothing remains. That we know more about the houses built in ancient Greece is due rather to their forms having been taken over and used by the Romans, their conquerors, than to the preservation of Greek domestic architecture.

The life of the Roman family was lived behind a barrier of high walls. Indeed, many of the houses in Pompeii have one story, one room and shops which back on to the wall on the outer face, isolating the house from the street. Entrance was normally through a single narrow door from the street, and the visitor then made his way through a series of courtyards which were encircled by pillars which supported the sloping roofs. In addition to the usual accommodation, each Roman house had a recessed area for the household gods and ancestral statues. Houses were not standardized: some had two or three stories, and there were tenements known as *insulae* and even bungalows. Large houses used rich marbles and other materials, but the ordinary citizen had to be content with walls of brick or tufa embedded in concrete and decorated with stucco painted to simulate more expensive materials. Small rooms could be made to appear larger by *trompe l'oeil* paintings, with artfully painted columns and alcoves, and even windows which appeared to open on to a wide landscape. Walls

A typical house of Pompeii, or Herculaneum.
Notice the emphasis on privacy.

59

The façade of a medieval house in France.

and floors were often of mosaic, with perhaps motifs derived from things used in the rooms—fruit and fish in the dining room, musical instruments in other rooms, and so on. Where necessary, houses were equipped with underfloor heating from a *hypocaust* in which hot gases from a furnace were circulated throughout the house.

Wherever the legions settled they transformed squalid tribal encampments into sophisticated towns, but these perished during the Dark Ages, and domestic architecture became more concerned with its defensive role. It was not until the fifteenth and sixteenth centuries that nobles in France ceased to be feudal overlords in fortified castles, and *maisons nobles* began to appear in towns.

Houses of this kind are normally built with a courtyard, with turretted stairways and an intricately ornamented façade forming the street entrance. The Hôtel de Cluny, now the Cluny Museum in Paris, or the Hôtel de Jacques Coeur in

Bourges are characteristic of the new medieval architecture. An exceptionally large and elaborate house which anticipates further developments is the Château de Blois, started by Louis XII but enlarged later, with a superb spiral staircase added by Francis I, in 1515–24. Many of these town houses, however, were erected in cities clustered within the obsolete city walls and they could find little ground upon which to expand. This, together with the prestige given by a high imposing façade, enforced vertical growth; houses of six or seven stories are found in many cities. In the Low Countries the encircling water-defenses which limited the expansion of towns resulted in high crow-stepped gabled houses which line the canals of Amsterdam, Ghent and other medieval cities.

In England, where defense was far less urgent than on the European mainland, scantily fortified manor houses such as Penshurst Place in Kent tended to sprawl outward. In Scotland, however, the restless lairds built high *tower-houses* or turretted and machicolated *houses of fence*.

The new medieval architecture. A crow-stepped gabled house in Delft (*left*). The spiral staircase at the Château de Blois, France (*right*).

The grandeur of the waterside palaces in Venice. The Doge's Palace is basically a Gothic structure. Note the lightness and elegance of design.

The effects of the collapse of the Roman Empire were, architecturally, not so severe in Spain, as the Moors who later occupied the Iberian peninsula brought with them an architectural richness which persisted for nearly 800 years. The Visigoths and Vandals were largely a woodworking people, but the Moors, who replaced them as rulers of the peninsula in the eighth century, were skilled craftsmen in stone, and Gothic houses in Spain have an Islamic exuberance of decoration surpassing anything on the continent of Europe at that time. The most famous secular building of this period is the Alhambra, in Granada, built in 1248–1354 as a home for Mahommed El Ghalib. This Moorish building resembled those he had already built in Jerusalem and Damascus. The piercing sunlight demanded that such medieval courtyards as those at the Palacio de la Audiencia and at the Casa del Ayuntamiento, both in Barcelona, be surrounded by a series of magnificent arcades not unlike the cloisters found in Gothic monasteries.

The form of a building is determined partly by its function

Moorish influences in Spanish architecture (1). Compare with the classical tradition of the Pisani in Venice (2).

and partly by the materials with which it is constructed. In Italy the wide range of building materials and resources of stone would alone have produced a variety of styles, even if the self-governing city-states had not been fiercely individual. Each evolved its own version of Gothic—that of Lombardy, with its rich brick and terracotta, is different from that of the other city-states like Milan, Florence, Lucca or Siena. Venice, a great maritime power, and Sicily, because of its proximity to the Near East, both adopted such Islamic features as the dome, and the Latin conquest of Byzantium was to enrich the architectural vocabulary of Italy even more.

The Doge's Palace, in Venice, despite later additions, is basically a Gothic structure of the early fourteenth century. The upper story of white and pink marble, diapered to suggest brickwork, is supported by a series of Gothic arcades, and the delicacy of the carved capitals could only have been carried out in marble, for other stones would have splintered. The Cà d'Oro and the Pisani Palace are two typically Vene-

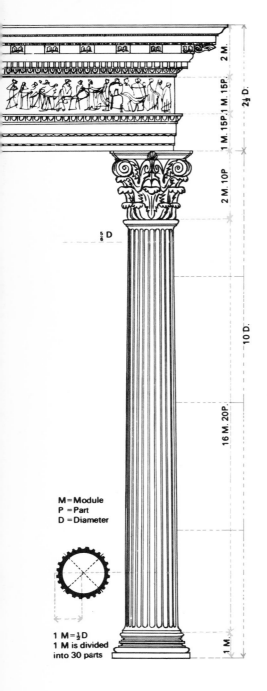

M = Module
P = Part
D = Diameter

1 M = ½D
1 M is divided
into 30 parts

An Order of Architecture, known as the 'Corinthian' order, in which the proportions of each member are most carefully related, mathematically.

tian Gothic buildings. For extreme examples of the motives of prestige and defense which forced houses higher and higher one should go to San Gimignano or Bologna.

The Gothic style, primarily a French 'invention' was never wholly acceptable to the Italians, who were always aware of their great, classical past; the Renaissance, therefore, appears first in Italy. To the Renaissance thinker, there was something improvised about the way in which Gothic buildings evolved. By comparison, the plan of a Renaissance house with its insistent symmetry, designed on a drawing board in every detail before one stone was cut, could be compared to the geometric perfection of a snow crystal, not the irregular development of an organism. One of the most obvious features which distinguishes the Renaissance from Gothic architecture is the use of the classical *Orders of Architecture,* a codified system of post-and-lintel construction used by the Greeks and developed by the Romans.

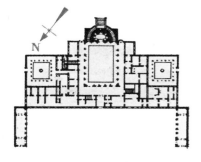

The façade of the Rucellai
Palace, Florence, (1446–51),
by Alberti, with plan of the
Pitti Palace, Florence, (c. 1440).

In an order of architecture the basic unit of measurement is a *module*, usually the radius of the circle at the base of a column. This was used to determine the relationships of the various parts of the column and the proportions of the architrave, frieze and cornice it supported. It determined the spaces between the columns, the proportion of parts of the building to each other and to the whole, relating them in a series of mathematical harmonies. The proportions of the *Doric* order differ from those of the *Ionic* or *Corinthian* orders but the basis of the system remains the same.

The Rucellai Palace, one of the first Renaissance buildings in Florence, was designed by the architect and writer Leon Battista Alberti in 1446. It vindicates the theories set out in Alberti's books in which he declared that the essence of beauty was 'the harmony and concord of all parts achieved in such a manner that nothing could be added, or taken away, or altered except for the worse'. His written works were to be the basis of a whole theory of architectural design.

The Pitti Palace, which Alberti might also have designed,

The Farnese Palace, Rome, (c. 1530).

is fashioned from huge blocks of stone, those on the ground floor being deliberately rough-hewn, a form of decoration known as *rustication*. The second story contains superb living quarters and is known as the *piano nobile*. Like the *piano nobile,* the uppermost story has paired windows and a huge overhanging cornice forming a serene roof line, uninterrupted by gables or turrets.

In plan, such houses are built symmetrically about a court, or *cortile*, which is usually surrounded by a cloister-like arcading, but the roof construction is now concealed by a plaster ceiling, heavily modeled or decorated with frescoes. The unit of scale is no longer the human figure, and doors and windows are designed to suit the mathematical proportions of the whole building. The construction of Venetian houses appears to be lighter than those of Florence, with open arcading and balconies enriching their façades with strong patterns of light and shade. Despite local variations, however, Italian Renaissance houses exhibit most characteristics of the Rucellai or the Pitti Palace.

Although Brunelleschi, the architect of the magnificent dome of Florence Cathedral, learned much from excavating the mighty classical ruins in Rome, the first Renaissance architect to work in Rome was Bramante. He was a Florentine friend of Alberti, who built the Palazzo della Cancellaria, planned on an irregular site but following the usual Renaissance pattern. Bramante wielded considerable influence and his pupils include Peruzzi, the architect of the Pietro Massimi Palace in Rome, Antonio da Sangallo the Younger, who designed the Farnese Palace in Rome, one of the most magnificent palaces in Europe, and Bramante's nephew, Raphael Santi, the painter.

Raphael's activities, like those of his great contemporaries Michelangelo and Leonardo da Vinci, included all kinds of interests apart from painting and architecture. He excavated the Baths of Titus and Nero's 'Golden House', and from these he was to derive a form of architectural decoration known as *grotteschi*. His 'Villa Madama' in Rome is a simple but elegant structure by comparison with the more ostentatious Pandolfini Palace in Florence built some 15 years later. Giacomo Barozzi da Vignola (1507–73) built his mighty fortress palace at Caprarola, the Farnese, but his widespread influence is not only due to his buildings but to his book *The Five Orders of Architecture*, a straightforward interpretation of the classical modular system published in 1562. Meanwhile, Michele Sanmichele and other north

The Cancelleria Palace, Rome, (1486–98).

Fontainebleau—one of the great
châteaux of France.

Italian architects were at work in Verona and in Venice,
using the classical orders as a point of departure for highly
original designs in a new style known as *Mannerist*, in which
the basic elements of classical composition were redisposed
quite unorthodoxically.

Of greater importance to domestic architecture, eventually, were buildings designed by Andrea Palladio, of Vicenza.
Palladio also trained in Rome, but his originality can be
seen in the Chiericati Palace which he erected in Vicenza in
1550, introducing a colonnaded loggia on its façade—an
innovation which later was to have far-reaching consequences
all over Europe. In such villas as the famous Villa Capra,
or 'Rotunda' because of its shallow dome, built in 1567, we
see for the first time precise mathematical relationships
applied not only to the façades but also to the proportions of
the rooms within.

In France the transition from Gothic to Renaissance was
less easy and initially consisted of trying to graft classical
forms onto virtually Gothic buildings. With an enclosed
courtyard for defense, larger windows demanded by the
climate, high chimney stacks and steeply pitched roofs, the
French château differed considerably from its counterpart in
Italy, despite the influence of such important Italians as
Vignola and Sebastiano Serlio, both of whom worked at
Fontainebleau.

It took some time for Italian Renaissance theories to reach

Section through the famous 'Rotunda' near Vicenza, Italy.

Paris, but in Flanders there was not only distance to be considered but also the violence of religious prejudice. Religious oppression had made the Flemings hostile to any ideas from Rome. Climatic and geological conditions, too, were very different. Steep roofs were essential to deal with rain and snow, and the clear stony forms of Italy had to be translated into forms suitable for brick. The patrons were merchants whose domestic architecture reflected their sober needs for a well-designed comfortable home. Classical ornament was acceptable as a surface decoration, but classical forms only if they

Façade of the Chiericati Palace.

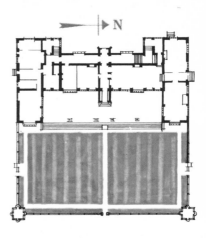

Plateresque decoration of the Casa del Ayuntamiento, Seville, Spain. Plan of 'Montecute', an Elizabethan house, showing its symmetry.

were adaptable to the practical demands of the house.

The Spanish occupation of the Netherlands made little practical difference to domestic architecture. In Spain itself, Renaissance architecture was further modifed by strong Moorish influences. Classical details were grafted onto primarily Gothic constructive forms, themselves already enriched with Islamic decoration. A rich surface ornamentation in stone, reminiscent of the hammered répousse work in silver, gave its name to a Spanish Renaissance style known as *Plateresque* (from *platero*, a silversmith). The Casa del Ayuntamiento in Seville has a façade which is typical of this kind.

Both in England and in Germany, early Renaissance buildings show the same unhappy superimposition of scarcely understood classical motifs on basically Gothic buildings, a state of affairs which lasted well into the sixteenth century. In England, most Elizabethan houses have an ornately carved screen and huge fireplace in the Great Hall, both lavishly decorated with motifs derived from pattern books such as those by Vredeman de Vries of Antwerp or Wendel Dietterlin of Strasbourg. A splendid staircase replaces the inconvenient spiral stairs and leads to the upper rooms where one important

The Great Staircase, Knole Park, Sevenoaks, England.

innovation is a multi-purpose room occupying the whole width of the house, known as the Long Gallery.

When the true Renaissance came to England, the inspiration was from Andrea Palladio and his exquisite villas around Vicenza visited by Inigo Jones, the English architect, and not from the Flemish pattern books. But even in Palladio's lifetime the Mannerist style, which had dealt so capriciously with classical rules, was to be succeeded by the *Baroque*, a style in which the movement of masses, the flow of space into space, and the fusion of painting, sculpture and architecture was to produce a style quite unlike the classical formality of the early Renaissance. Although it was particularly effective in producing high emotional tension in church architecture, it produced some magnificent domestic buildings. The oval plan, with its greater possibility for longitudinal expansion, replaced the more rigid one based on the circle and the square. The landscape itself was brought into a more intimate relationship with the swirling forms of the buildings and the curving staircases and colonnades.

In Italy the chief exponent of Baroque was the Neapolitan painter, sculptor and architect, Gianlorenzo Bernini, whose

Palazzo Odescalchi—a palace of the Italian Baroque.

most important secular buildings in Rome are the Montecitorio
Palace, built from 1650 onward, and the Odescalchi Palace,
erected somewhat after 1644. A former assistant of his,
Francesco Borromini, was his chief rival, but neither Borromini's buildings nor the secular ones of another rival,
Pietro Cortone, compare with Bernini's. In Venice, as in Rome,
the development into Baroque is less evident among palaces
than among the churches, and the Pesaro Palace by Baldassare
Longhena is the only one markedly Baroque.

The traditionally exuberant nature of Spanish architecture
made Baroque welcome, and its exponents were mainly three
brothers, José, Joaquín and Alberto Churriguera, whose
lavish application of carved surface decoration gave rise to a
version of the Baroque known as *Churrigueresque*, a style the
more complex because of the added influence of native art
from Spanish overseas possessions.

A more restrained form of Baroque was made more acceptable in France through the writings of Du Cerceau the Elder, whose book *Les plus excellents bastiments de France* was published in the years 1576 and 1579. Bernini himself was invited to redesign the Louvre, and work began under his direction in 1665, but it was eventually completed by Le Brun, the painter, and an amateur architect, Claude Perrault. Although the Baroque style was particularly suitable for the complex establishments housing the kings of France and their vast retinues, its effect was also apparent in great landscape gardens such as that by Le Nôtre at Versailles. In Valognes, the Hôtel de Beaumont, with its sinuously curving façade, is a good example of a provincial Baroque house, but the style was too large to be used for ordinary domesticity. From the lithe movement of its curves, however, the French developed a form of interior decoration known as *Rococo*, a light witty style more readily absorbed into small houses than the more ponderous Baroque.

Neither style found much response in England. Almost the only secular Baroque buildings in England, Castle Howard and Blenheim Palace, were both built by Sir John Vanbrugh, the playwright-architect, and neither exhibit the lavish freedom of movement associated with the Baroque in other parts of the continent of Europe.

A great French town house—the Hôtel Soubise, Paris.

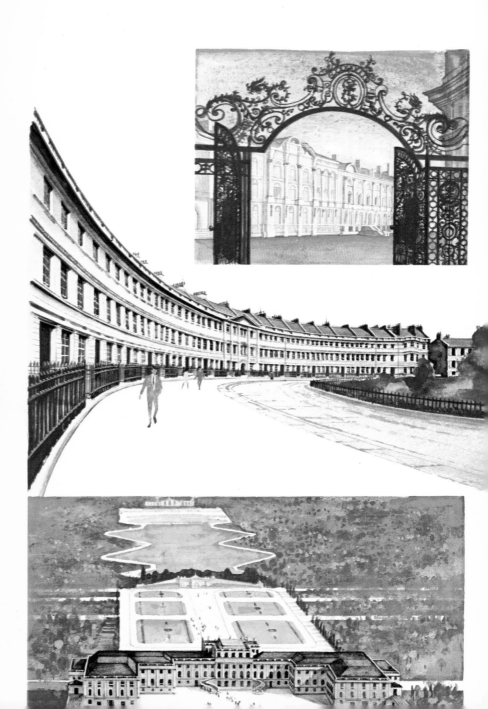

Early in the eighteenth century, Peter the Great decided to bring Russia architecturally in line with the rest of Europe. He employed foreign architects, and his vast palace at St. Petersburg was intended to be a second Versailles. The most important architect in Russia by the middle of the century was a Venetian, Bartolomeo Rastrelli. He was employed by the Empress Elizabeth to build the palace of Tsarskoe Selo in the Baroque style, and later to work on the Winter Palace at St. Petersburg.

A comparable palace in size and beauty in Vienna, the Schönbrunn, was designed originally by a Venetian-trained Austrian, J. B. Fischer von Erlach. Von Erlach's chief rival, Johann Lukas von Hildebrandt, used a lighter and even more fantastic version of Baroque when he produced the Upper Belvedere Palace for Prince Eugène. Superb curved staircases and vaulting appear to be supported by writhing 'supermen' of stone, with the exaggerated gesture of the Grand Opera.

Such dramatic effects might suit absolute monarchs, but away in Holland a more reticent Palladian style was used for the Mauritshuis in The Hague, designed in 1633 for Prince John Maurits of Nassau by Jacob van Campen. This style was indeed preferred all over Europe to the more extravagant Baroque. The arrival in England of William of Orange from Holland confirmed the Englishman's preference for this kind of Palladianism, and English architects began to develop it not only for country houses, but also for whole streets of houses with one unified Palladian façade. The temporary residents of Bath and other 'spa' towns accepted the architectural discipline imposed by John Wood and his son as readily as they bowed to the will of Beau Nash in the Assembly Rooms, and in doing so allowed them to create some of the loveliest street architecture in Europe. Each house bore an organized mathematical relationship to the whole street, and the same care was exercised in every part of the house. Every detail down to the proportion of the cornices and fireplaces followed a series of pre-ordained proportions.

Gateway, the Palace of Tsarskoe Selo, Russia. The classical formality of an English eighteenth-century crescent. The grandeur of the continental palace and garden, (Schönbrunn, Vienna).

Books published under the patronage of Lord Burlington, the leader of the Palladians in England, did not, as Pope had feared, 'Fill half the land with imitating fools', but together with books written by such architects and designers as James Gibbs, Robert Adam and Thomas Chippendale, they made it possible for beautifully and 'correctly' designed houses to appear in every part of the country. Unlike his French counterpart, whose attendance at court increased the importance of his town house, the Englishman lavished his attention on his country house — his true home, where he could cultivate his lands or breed magnificent beasts. He only came to town grudgingly when business or Parliament required him. Discoveries at Herculaneum and Pompeii gave further impetus to the interest in classical architecture, and Winckelmann's *History of Ancient Art*, published in 1763, introduced Grecian architecture to architects previously obsessed with Roman buildings. Unfortunately, all this antiquarianism tended to deflect architects from the need for practical functional plans for their houses.

By the end of the century a demand for variety brought widely dissimilar elements to the architectural scene, and 'Egyptian', 'Chinese' and 'Moorish/Hindu' decorations were imported or invented to clothe basically classical buildings. By the middle of the nineteenth century architectural decoration had become a rag-bag of details looted willy-nilly from the proliferating textbooks on historic ornament, and John

Chiswick House, the 'Palladian' villa in England.

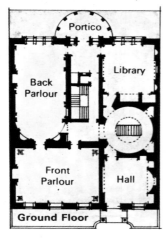
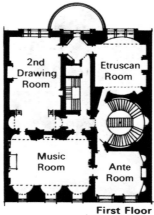

Ground Floor — Portico, Back Parlour, Library, Front Parlour, Hall

First Floor — 2nd Drawing Room, Etruscan Room, Music Room, Ante Room

Above: Plans of a typical Georgian town house.
Below: Kedleston, Derbyshire; a mid-eighteenth-century country-house, largely by Robert Adam. The garden front.

Ruskin was to confirm architects in their error by declaring 'architecture is ornament applied to building'.

In England the unity of street architecture preserved by the Adam brothers and continued by John Nash disappeared as streets developed into strings of unrelated detached or semi-detached houses, each an extravagant travesty of a bygone age. All over Europe, ill-designed boxes with subterranean kitchens masqueraded as 'Greek' temples or 'Venetian Gothic' castles with spires ten feet high. Each country drew its

inspiration from its own past. The châteaux of the Loire and the great epoch of 'Le Roi Soleil' provided France with her inspiration, while the newly formed German states wavered between a debased Baroque, spiky 'Schloss' architecture, or timber-framing as spurious as the black-letter printing which had become the official German typeface.

In England the architectural taste was equally confused. The Middle Ages, suitably romanticized in the novels of Sir Walter Scott, inspired the *Gothic Revival*, while the presence of the young Queen Victoria stimulated interest in the architecture of Queen Elizabeth and the Tudor period in general. Thus an embittered conflict sprung up between a faction who wished to recreate the glories of the Middle Ages and sixteenth-century England and their opponents to whom the only possible architecture was that of classical Greece and Rome. The evolution of new techniques, which made the Crystal Palace possible, and the new methods demonstrated by such engineers as Brunel and Telford, which might have transformed nineteenth-century architecture, were almost entirely ignored by architects obsessed with the external appearance of their buildings. By the end of the century the British had settled for a 'decent' unadventurous domestic architecture which harked back somewhat to the sobriety of Queen Anne and the Georges. The initiative which the English held in industry failed to be maintained by the architects and passed to those of other countries who, taking advantage of British technical achievements, created a truly living architecture from them. One of the few really original British architects, Charles Rennie Mackintosh, ignored by the native patrons of architecture, was feted in Austria, and his ideas were seized and exploited by more appreciative foreign architects.

Some architects reacted violently against the slavish imitation of out-moded forms by trying to create entirely new ones without architectural precedent. In England Charles Voysey succeeded in producing houses which were humane

(1) A nineteenth-century country house combining different historic styles. (2) The clarity and honesty of a house by C. R. Mackintosh. (3) Cornelius Vanderbilt House, New York City; an example of Victorian architecture.

1

2

3

Apartment house in the Rue
Franklin, Paris, showing early
use of reinforced concrete,
(1903). Diagram of slab
construction by reinforced
concrete, Le Corbusier, (1914).

in scale and comely in appearance, but he stood almost alone.
Apart from the extravagantly original forms of building
emerging from the unique and ebullient Antoni Gaudi in
Spain, there is little to be found in Europe.

Few people had realized that using steel or reinforced concrete framing made the walls of the building, as weight-
bearing members, unnecessary. The wall in such a house was
little more than a weatherproof screen hanging like a curtain
from the edge of the framework, or acting as a partition inside,
to be moved about at will. Freed from the necessity to place
his walls structurally, the architect could treat the whole
interior space of the house much more freely, and American
architect Frank Lloyd Wright was demonstrating the practi-
cality of this *open-plan* technique in Illinois as early as 1901.

The traditional pitched roof, however, was also an inhibit-
ing factor in the development of an intricate plan. With the
development of reinforced concrete slabs, it was realized that
no matter now involved the shape of a building, a reinforced
concrete lid could always be evolved to cover it. Frank Lloyd

Wright's early rivals were to be found in France. Following Hennebique's experiments with reinforced concrete, the Perret brothers realized that here was not just a cheap substitute for stone but a new building material with immense potential of its own. In 1903 a block of apartments designed by Auguste Perret was erected in the Rue Franklin, in Paris—the first ever to be made of reinforced concrete.

In Germany the establishment of the Deutscher Werkbund in 1907 was to lead to the investigation of architectural planning and to force architects to make a reappraisal of traditional ways of designing houses. It is true that architects such as Walter Gropius, Adolph Meyer and Peter Behrens were more concerned initially with the application of the new materials and techniques to the design of industrial architecture, or to the accommodation of workers in large housing schemes, but acceptance of these new materials and the original forms which appeared were made much easier by their success.

World War I and the economic chaos which followed proved to be only a temporary check to architectural experiment. Indeed, the necessity for impoverished nations to make the most of their technical resources, together with the breathing space which uneasy neutrality had allowed to Switzerland, Holland and the Scandinavian countries gave something of an

Robie House, Chicago, Illinois, by Frank Lloyd Wright (1909).

impetus to architecture all over Europe which might have been lacking in a less urgent situation.

After the war, Walter Gropius, who had been a pupil of Behrens, took over the Bauhaus, a school of industrial design and of architectural research in Weimar. He later transferred it to Dessau, housing it in a magnificent building of his own creation that embodied all the principles of the new architecture. In 1930 he left it in the hands of Ludwig Mies van der Rohe, also a pupil of Behrens, and eventually spent some time in England (1934–36), where he collaborated with a brilliant English architect, Maxwell Fry.

In the meantime, another pupil of Behrens, Charles Edouard Jeanneret, a Swiss architect, better known as Le Corbusier, set up independently in 1922. His much mis-quoted definition 'a house is a machine for living in' is demonstrated by such houses as that designed at Garches in 1927, but his world-wide influence does not rest by any means on the buildings he created, but on his tremendously stimulating books on architecture and town-planning. *Vers une Architecture* of 1922, and *Urbanisme*, produced in 1924, have dominated almost every major architectural development during the last 40 years. Since this section is primarily concerned with domestic architecture, the wide range of buildings designed by this brilliant and provocative architect cannot possibly be covered. Mention must be made, however, of his huge residential scheme near Marseilles, a vertical village to house 1,600 people, known as the 'Unité d'Habitation', and of his more recent planning in the Punjab at Chandigarh, in which he collaborated with Maxwell Fry and Jane Drew.

Houses such as the Farnsworth House in Plano, Illinois, show that although Mies van der Rohe insisted on all his students at the Illinois Institute undergoing the most rigorous investigation of the qualities inherent in the traditional materials and construction in wood, stone and brick, he is prepared to use the more modern methods. Thus he uses steel frame and sheet glass with exquisite sensitivity.

(1) Maison Stein at Garches, France, by Le Corbusier, (1927).
(2) Plan of a house by Mies van der Rohe. (3) Diagram showing excessive development of a cantilever, (the Schminke House, Lobau, 1932).

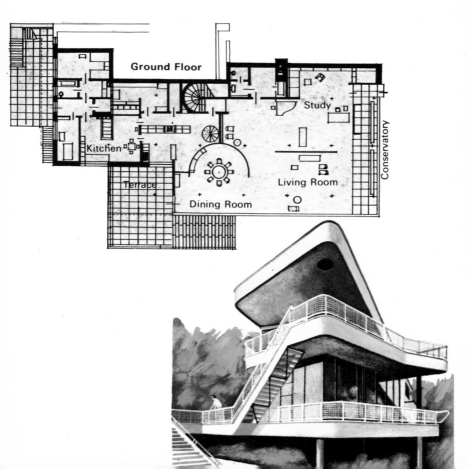

Ground Floor

Kitchen

Terrace

Dining Room

Study

Living Room

Conservatory

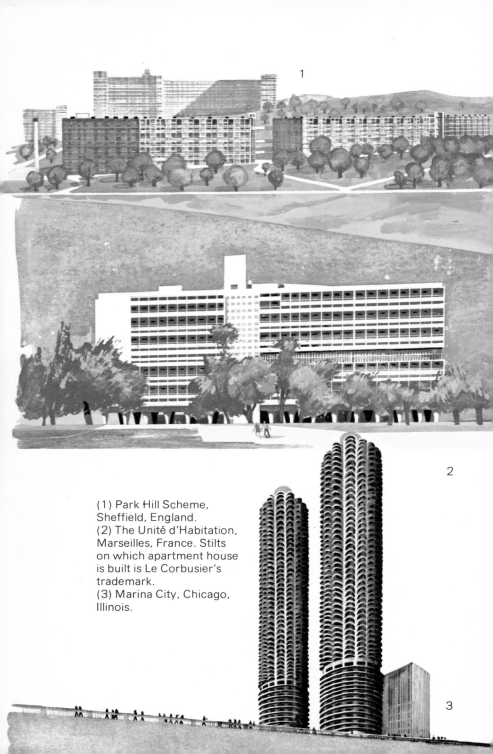

(1) Park Hill Scheme,
Sheffield, England.
(2) The Unité d'Habitation,
Marseilles, France. Stilts
on which apartment house
is built is Le Corbusier's
trademark.
(3) Marina City, Chicago,
Illinois.

It is interesting to compare this house with another, built some ten years later at Taliesin West, Arizona, by his rival and critic Frank Lloyd Wright. The Farnsworth House has a finely wrought steel frame which pares the construction away so that it scarcely exists, visually. At Taliesin West, Wright has used the construction and harsh surface quality of reinforced concrete so that it is insistent, almost clamorous, throughout every part of the house.

Houses such as these are, in a sense, freaks, and a very long way from the acute problem of providing houses in large numbers for the dispossessed and homeless in every part of the world. Nevertheless, it is through the freedom allowed by the design of such houses that many architects have made technical advances, just as the family car, eventually, benefits from the 'freak' cars which race at the Monte Carlo Rally. Mies van der Rohe himself is well aware of this. He superintended a most influential exhibition of the Deutscher Werkbund in Stuttgart as early as 1927, in which such men as Peter Behrens, Walter Gropius, Le Corbusier and the Dutch architect J. J. P. Oud concentrated on the design of houses in which a degree of standardization would make it possible for them to be produced economically from units manufactured on the factory floor and assembled on the site.

The rebuilding of the shattered cities of Europe after World War II again emphasized the need for the full use of industrial techniques in the building industry and the necessity for these to be understood and applied by trained and sensitive architects. Typical of the new approach in France is the town of Bagnols-sur-Cèze, built under the direction of a former pupil of Le Corbusier, a Russian named Georges Candilis. In Holland, such architects as J. H. van den Broek and Jacob B. Bakema have been active, despite opposition from 'traditionalists', in the rebuilding of Rotterdam.

Despite certain shortages, neutral Sweden and Switzerland were able to develop their own architectural techniques during the war. The Gröndal Estate in Stockholm, by Sven Backstrom and Leif Reinius, shows a more humane approach to communal housing, while in Switzerland the tradition of the famous Neubühl estate, built in Zurich in 1930–32, still continues in such housing schemes as that at the Gellert district, in Basle, and the Halen estate, near Berne. Perhaps the high cylindrical towers of Marina City, Chicago, or the cubical blocks of 'Habitat' at the Expo '67 exhibition in Montreal will become a feature of future European cities.

Recent developments in such processes as I.B.I.S. (industrial building in steel) and other forms of industrialized housing show that more has yet to be done before it is to be accepted by many architects and the public they serve. They fear that such techniques are as likely to mass-produce badly designed houses as well as well-designed ones, unless strict control is exercised on those responsible for the design processes. Prejudice against industrialized housing may be due, in part, to the appearance of 'pre-fabs', small temporary homes erected after World War II for bombed-out families, which were in use far longer than was originally intended. These houses have weathered badly, but they are far better planned internally than some houses being built by traditional methods today.

Some critics of industrialized housing envisage a torrent of 'dwelling units', all exactly alike, pouring from the assembly lines and invading the countryside, inflicting as much damage

The industrialized house—a series of diagrams showing its assembly. Erection of prefabricated walls on the prepared foundation; services are installed; plumbing; fittings; and the house at its completion.

as the grim factory towns of the Industrial Revolution or the suburban sprawl of the 1930's. Industrialized housing must be developed, however, if slum-clearance schemes are to be implemented and the world-wide shortage of homes is to be met. With houses being constructed under cover by machine tools and a minimum of work needed on the site, six houses can be ready for occupation in under a week and blocks of apartment houses have been built from pre-fabricated house-units in a tenth of the time required by more traditional methods. By careful planning it is possible to construct a house in such a way that it can be readily extended by the addition of new room-units as the family grows, or adapted to changing circumstances as the children grow up and finally leave home. There is even talk of 'built-in obsolescence' by which homes may be used for a certain length of time, and then 'traded in' like an obsolete car. To add to the problem of the disposal of unwanted cars, that of obsolete homes, made from virtually indestructible materials like plastics, may well be something against which we shall have to be on our guard, but at present, there is no danger of over-production of homes in the forseeable future.

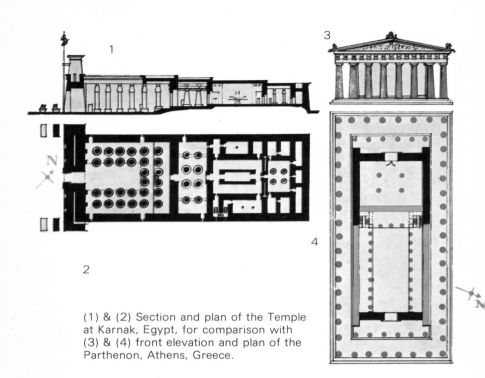

(1) & (2) Section and plan of the Temple at Karnak, Egypt, for comparison with (3) & (4) front elevation and plan of the Parthenon, Athens, Greece.

Buildings for Worship

The planning of buildings designed for worship will obviously vary according to the rituals evolved by different religions. It is not enough that a Christian church should offer shelter to a congregation or have facilities for music and a pulpit. It must also be sufficiently large and emotionally impressive to make it worthy of being 'God's house'.

Many religious buildings, however, were not expected to provide accommodation for large congregations, but were intended to be the setting for holy mysteries carried out by a priesthood hierarchy, at which privileged worshippers might be present as passive spectators. It was this type of worship which determined the design of such temples as that of Amun at Karnak, in Egypt, whose basic plan evolved over some 2,000 years, as successive Pharaohs added their own extensions, increasing its sense of power and terror. The whole building is designed to proclaim the omnipotence of the god-king to whom it is dedicated and to terrify the mortal who dares to enter it.

An entirely different concept of religion in Greece had produced by the fifth century B.C. an entirely different kind of temple—a precious casket or shrine to house the sacred statue of the god and the priesthood who ministered to it, not a church to shelter the worshippers. Many experimental versions of this kind of temple appeared before the Parthenon, erected by Ictinus and Callicrates in 447–432 B.C. But this small building, about 100 feet wide and 200 feet long, is the essence of all the refinements of mathematical proportion evolved over hundreds of years.

Roman temples closely followed the Greek pattern, but most are considerably larger than those of Greece. They display superior engineering skill by the vaulting of the roofs of the main rooms, or *cellas,* and favor the more ornate Corinthian Order for the columnar construction. Roman temples are to be found in every part of the Empire, in Baalbek, Palmyra, North Africa, and throughout Europe. The circular form of the Pantheon may well have been derived from Etruscan ancestry, and

'El Castillo', at Chichén Itzá, Yucatan, Mexico.

Early buildings for worship: Buddhist stupa at Sanchi, India.

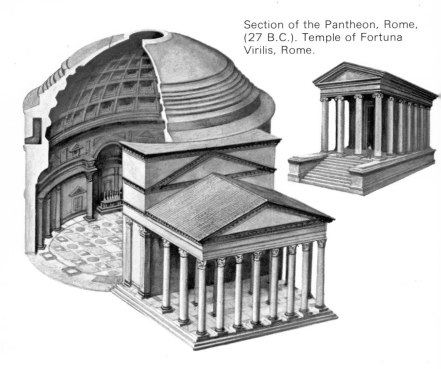

Section of the Pantheon, Rome, (27 B.C.). Temple of Fortuna Virilis, Rome.

the magnificently coffered dome of brickwork held with thick mortar is over 140 feet in diameter, supported on concrete walls 20 feet thick. The walls within are clad with marble and porphyry and hold a succession of niches for the statues of gods and altars for their worship. The building is lit by one huge central unglazed 'eye' in the dome—an immensely dramatic and emotional source of light.

The form of the Buddhist *stupas* in India, which were virtually shrines containing relics, differs radically from that of the Pyramid of the Sun, in Mexico, or the Maya temple known as El Castillo, at Chichén Itzá, because the religious requirements were totally different. The architectural requirements of the Muslim faith were extremely simple. The worshippers needed a cool and secluded place for prayer and contemplation, facilities for ablutions, a pulpit from which sermons could be preached, a raised platform from which portions of the Koran were recited, and some indication on the wall of the direction of Mecca to which they should turn while praying. Later, accommodation was provided for scholars and their pupils, for Muslim educational buildings were usually in close relationship with the mosque.

The mosque builders used the arch both as a decorative and as a constructional unit in simple semicircular, pointed and more elaborate cusped forms and were equally at home with the construction of arches and domes in bricks or in stone. Wall surfaces were faced with magnificent tiles or carvings, but the faith forbade representational art, particularly the representation of human and animal forms, and the tendency was to smother all wall surfaces with intricate linear but non-figurative patterns. An essential element of the building was also a tower, or *minaret,* from which the muezzin called the faithful to prayer.

The needs of the early Christians were even more simple than those of the Muslims. While they were still a persecuted minority they needed little more than a room in which to

Mohammed Ali Mosque, Cairo. A great Muslim mosque with minarets from which to call the faithful to prayer.

worship. After their faith had become an official religion, the Roman basilicas which they adapted retained much of the former simplicity and a closer contact between priest and laity than became possible in later churches.

Like the mosque, the early Christian church had a fountain for ceremonial cleansing before worship. This fountain is the central focus of the open court which, surrounded by cloisters, forms the entrance to the church precinct that worshippers crossed before entering the *narthex,* or porch, leading into the body of the church. The altar is not necessarily at the eastern end, and in S. Clemente, in Rome, a typical early Christian church, it is at the western end. Here the space reserved for the choir projects well into the nave, and is surrounded by a low wall. One side supports an *ambo,* or pulpit, from which the gospel was read, and an opposite side supports a second ambo for the Epistle. The altar, which is free-standing, is immediately to the rear of the choir, and the bishop's chair is in an *apse,* or semicircular recess, behind the altar. During the first part of the service the priests would occupy the apse, but during the Eucharist the bread and wine were brought to the altar by the laity before being accepted, blessed and administered by the priests. The absence of any substantial barrier between priest and laity emphasizes that this is an act of corporate worship, an arrangement which was later lost. The nave is flanked by aisles, and the *clerestory* windows above them light the whole church. In early churches, the timber roof spanning the nave was exposed, but later this was often concealed with plaster coffering.

Not all churches followed this plan. Some were round or octagonal. The largest round church is probably S. Stefano Rotondo in Rome, while certainly one of the most beautiful of octagonal churches must be S. Vitale, in Ravenna. Like so many churches of this period, S. Vitale has a sumptuous interior, with walls encased in glittering mosaic set in a background of iridescent gold, and with capitals of nacreous marble pierced and fretted with intricate patterns.

The most important of all Byzantine churches, Santa Sophia, was erected in A.D. 532–537 in Istanbul which was then called Byzantium. It was the most splendid church in Christendom. The vaulting construction, normally found in contemporary

The interior of San Clemente,
an early Christian church in
Rome. A pierced marble capital
from San Vitale, Ravenna, Italy.
A section through San Vitale.

architecture, is augmented by a dome construction derived from the Middle East, with Roman brick and concrete techniques developed into a complex system of construction unsuspected by the original inventors. The main body of the church, without its double narthex, is approximately 220 feet square and cruciform. Outside, the brick walls are almost plain, but within, walls and piers are clad in sheets of multicolored marbles from North Africa and the Middle East. The floors are inlaid with mosaics of colored marble, and the brick vaults and domes are furnished with glittering glass mosaics set in a golden background.

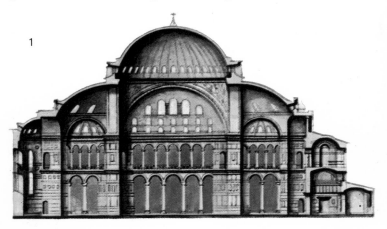

1

Santa Sophia is unique, but its dome construction appears in a modified form in many smaller churches in Asia Minor — in the little Metropole Cathedral, Athens, for example, where the dome is raised on a drum, and in other Greek Orthodox churches, where the simple service and absence of instrumental music demanded little more than a tiny cruciform room with a central dome, under which the worshippers could stand.

The influence of Byzantine domed architecture is apparent as far away as Venice, where the churches represent a fusion between the cultures of East and West. Russian churches of this period also resemble those of Byzantium, but whereas the latter are invariably of brick or stone, most of the Russian ones are of wood. They are small in scale, with window areas reduced to the minimum, because of the extremes of heat and cold. In many the narthex is replaced by a *trapeza*, a low chamber which provided shelter and warmth for worshippers, and which was isolated from the main body of the church by a thick, brick wall pierced with slit windows through which the service could be followed. An elaborately carved screen, or *iconostasis*, separates the small nave from the chancel. The most striking development outside is the evolution of the onion-shaped dome from the simple Byzantine one, and its use, not only over the center of the church but on many semi-circular apses.

While Byzantine traditions continued in the East, western

2

(1) A section through Santa Sophia, Istanbul, Turkey. (2) A church of the Greek Orthodox faith, Daphni, Greece. (3) A Russian church, Byzantine in form, but not necessarily in date.

3

(1) The west front of
St. Trophîme, Arles.
(2) St. Pierre, Angoulême,
showing some of the
characteristics of the churches
on the pilgrimage routes.

Europe, subjected to a series of invasions, was plunged into
the Dark Ages. The architecture which emerged toward
A.D. 1000, primitive though it was, reached back through
Byzantium to Rome itself for its inspiration, and is therefore
called *Romanesque*. The impact of Roman forms on Romanesque churches is more obvious in areas where substantial
remnants of Roman architecture survived. At Arles the west
front of St. Trophîme is clearly derived from a Roman triumphal arch, freely adapted to a Christian church. The decorative
use of classical details, however, is not so important as the
rediscovery by early Gothic builders of the constructional
principles and their development of them. Because the Church
was truly Catholic—that is, universal—important developments of this kind were widely disseminated. The use of the
dome is common enough in Italy (St. Mark's, Venice) and in
southwestern France (Angoulême, Fontevrault) but rare
further north. Sheathing walls in parti-colored marble, as at
Pisa, is confined to Italy, and where the region is closely linked

with Islamic culture, as in Sicily, this modified the appearance of even Christian churches.

Of the timber *stave* churches of Scandinavia, one built at Borgund, in Norway, in 1150, still survives. It is simple in plan, with a high, narrow nave covered by a deeply pitched timber roof and lit by clerestory windows cut in the side walls immediately over the roofs of the narrow aisles. Stone and brick churches in Scandinavia were subject to diverse influences. Cluniac monks first brought Christianity to Scandinavia, and the early churches owe a good deal to those of Burgundy. Later, under the Cistercians, the churches were more severely decorated and frugally furnished, and during the thirteenth century the preaching friars introduced the simple *hall-church* plan, in which the nave and aisles were of about the same height.

The most powerful stabilizing factor in the survival of European culture during the Dark Ages was indeed the monastery, a tightly knit community, able not only to preserve the European cultural heritage, but to develop it. The plan of

S. Maria Novella, Florence, showing inlaid marble facade.

a monastery and its ancillary buildings shows with what intelligence and sensitivity all the complex activities of such a community were integrated architecturally. The great church dominates the plan, but it was realized that man is a trinity of spirit, mind and body and that the needs of each must be met if perfect harmony is to be achieved. The plans vary slightly from one monastic order to another and are modified according to the geographical limitations of the site. As churches differed somewhat in function, plans were modified accordingly. Those for the orders of friars were primarily large halls in which worshippers assembled to hear the preaching. These were, ideally, without aisles and needed only plenty of space, an altar and a pulpit, a type of plan which, in Germany, was the prototype of the hall churches of the later periods. Huge churches, such as those at Vézelay and Poitou, on the pilgrimage route from France to Santiago de Compostela in Spain, were specially designed to deal with vast numbers of temporary worshippers, and here the apsidal end is developed into separate chapels capable of handling large congregations in smaller groups.

During the Middle Ages, the Church was the powerhouse of intellectual development, and it is in its building that are found the most remarkable technical innovations. The substitution of a ribbed vault for the groined one, and the development of the pointed arch, which appeared almost simultaneously at Durham and in Normandy, led to the most revolutionary systems of construction known. Whereas all previous methods had depended on dead weight being supported by inert mass, the Gothic builders evolved a dynamic method by which the weight of the roof was transferred through ribbed vaults to selected points on the walls and along buttresses to the ground. The buildings are maintained by a series of brilliantly controlled tensions held in equilibrium, and this architectural victory over technical difficulties is made to

(1) Fountains Abbey, Yorkshire, showing the relationship of church to cloisters and other buildings.
(2) A stave-church of wood from Borgund, Norway, (c. 1150).

(3) The interior of St. Denis near Paris, designed by Abbot Suger, and consecrated in 1144.
(4) Detail of a Celtic Cross, (Murdoch's Cross), Monasterboice, Ireland.

1

2

3

4

The apse of a French Gothic church at Bourges.

express the most intense religious feeling and to produce buildings of breathtaking beauty.

Gothic architecture is primarily a French creation, but since France in the twelfth century comprised little more than the area around Paris, all the other self-governing provinces might claim that the architecture evolving there was equally French. Nevertheless, it was in the Île de France that the full possibilities of the Gothic revolution were first realized and perfected. At St. Denis, north of Paris, Abbot Suger first devised the arrangement of small apses at the east ends of the pilgrimage churches to provide chapels for large numbers of pilgrims.

It was from the Île de France, too, that architectural emissaries went to Italy, Spain, Germany and finally England, spreading the doctrine of Gothic construction. Italy accepted it with reluctance, for here the classical tradition was too firmly entrenched, and her Gothic period was prematurely overtaken by the Renaissance. Elsewhere in the evolution of Gothic architecture we can detect versions which we can conveniently label German Gothic, Spanish Gothic or English Gothic—national variations on the main theme. Broadly, German Gothic is nearer to French than the others, but the churches of northern Germany, being of brick, differ from their French counterparts. Whereas others often have a nave and aisles of equal height and a single western tower or a western apse instead of the familiar French frontage with twin towers and wide sculpture-framed doorways. Spanish Gothic yields to Moorish influence with an excess of ornament and the horseshoe arch.

In England, Gothic cathedrals favor a great central tower over the crossing of the nave and transepts, and the latter project more widely than those of a French cathedral. The English preferred a square rather than a apsidal end at the west and, to French eyes, an excessively long nave. The close that surrounds most English cathedrals disappeared in France under a welter of secular buildings, and there are other less obvious differences. Because of the comparative

(1) The interior of Amiens Cathedral, France. (2) The vast window of Gloucester Cathedral, with wall areas pared to the minimum.

2

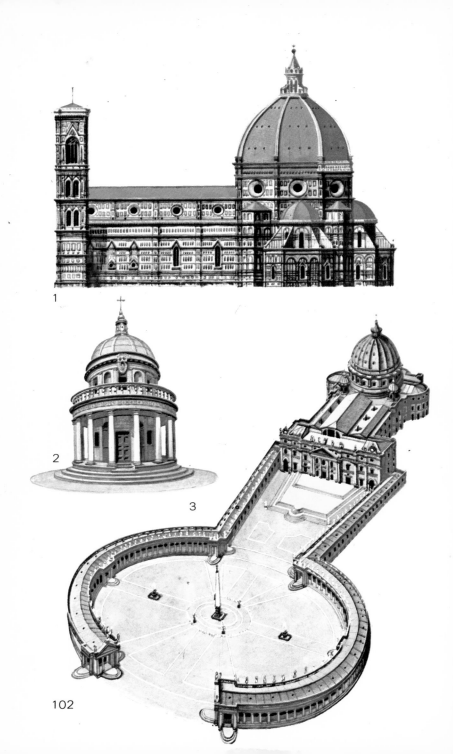

1

2

3

102

isolation of England from the architectural movements on the mainland of Europe in the fifteenth century the English went on to evolve a very personal type of architecture in the so-called *Perpendicular* period. English churches became great birdcages of stone through a refinement of construction unequalled anywhere in Europe which, by then, was experiencing the first wave of the Renaissance spreading outward from Italy.

Unless one had lived in Italy in the thirteenth century, speaking a language deeply rooted in Latin and surrounded by constant reminders of a great classical past, it is difficult to imagine how the Italians could have jettisoned the whole technical system of Gothic architecture and substituted the static calm of a bygone age for the tensions and excitement of soaring columns and vaults and flying buttresses.

Although the remembrance of the classical traditions had never been entirely submerged even during the Gothic period, it had survived in Italy more vividly than anywhere else in Europe, to the virtual exclusion of Gothic ideals. The rediscovery of classical literature, the encouragement given to the new learning by Florentine and Venetian nobles and Roman popes were all factors in the development of Renaissance architecture.

Gothic construction, with its abolition of the wall and its emphasis on wide window areas, was unsuitable for a country where windows had to be restricted to exclude the glare of the sun and where wall surfaces were vehicles for magnificent frescoes. Almost the only Gothic feature to be retained was the dome, and this was to be transformed by such architects as Filippo Brunelleschi, at Florence, and by Donato Bramante in his delightful Tempietto, in Rome, and later with the magnificence of Michelangelo's dome which crowns the mighty cathedral church of St. Peter. For the rest, the exposed Gothic vault was rejected in favor of the huge barrel vaults of the classical buildings, and the clustered piers replaced by the mathematical exactness of the Orders of Architecture promulgated by Vitruvius. The restless skyline

(1) The exterior of Florence Cathedral, (1296–1461). (2) The Tempietto, Rome, by Bramante, (1502). (3) St. Peter's, Rome— dome by Michelangelo and colonnades by Bernini.

(1) San Carlo alle Quattro Fontane, Rome, by Borromini, (1667).
(2) Sta Maria della Salute, Venice, (1631–85); Baroque exuberance.

of crocket and spire gave way to the Olympian calm of architrave, frieze and cornice. The somewhat organic growth of
many of the Gothic churches was anathema to the purists of the
Renaissance, and churches were now made to be mathematically proportioned so that any addition or subtraction of any
part would be ruinous to the harmonious relationship of the
whole building.

As the High Renaissance approached, much of the serenity
began to disappear. An intellectual restlessness and wilfulness
began to replace the calm of the earlier period, and although
classical details continued to be used, they were handled in a
wayward fashion quite unlike the truly classical buildings.
Such churches as San Carlo alle Quattro Fontane, in Rome,
carried out over a period of over 30 years, has a complicated plan
originally derived from a Greek cross, but so distorted that this
is by no means apparent. The undulating façade was carried
out just before Francesco Borromini's suicide in 1667. Architecture became increasingly a matter of the expression of the
individual architect or the whim of his patrons. The unity

The interior of St. Étienne du Mont, Paris, showing the famous 'jube' or staircase; a mixture of Gothic and Renaissance.

which we find in the Gothic ideals gave way to a more fragmented theory of architectural form, and the penetration of Renaissance architectural ideas was more liable to be affected by religious or political considerations than architectural ones.

The Roman Catholic countries least affected by the Reformation continued to develop their own national styles of Renaissance architecture and from thence to evolve Mannerist and Baroque versions. In Venice, for example, the restraint of the Mannerist church of San Giorgio, designed by Andrea Palladio in 1567, can be compared with the more exuberant Baroque of Sta Maria della Salute, designed by the Roman architect Baldassare Longhena in 1632. Early buildings in France betray a certain uneasiness. St. Étienne du Mont in Paris is a strange combination of Gothic and Renaissance details, and it is not until the church of the Val-de-Grâce (1645–50) or the church of the Sorbonne, that we find any assurance in the French architects in the handling of Renaissance details.

It is ironical that St. Peter's in Rome, one of the greatest monuments of the Renaissance thought, should have been indirectly responsible for the Reformation, a revolution which, whatever its religious results, was to be architecturally catastrophic in those countries in which it took place. The lavish expenditure on St. Peter's caused the sale of indulgences to be increased, and this in turn led to the famous protest by Luther which was to spark off the Reformation. The damage to the Gothic churches of England and the Netherlands was irreplaceable. Magnificent sculptures were hewn down, the great stained-glass windows lay in glittering ruins on the scarred pavements, and the carved rood screens were wrenched out. When comparative peace returned, the churches had to be entirely re-designed and any new ones planned to accommodate an entirely different type of religious service. The Reformation delayed the acceptance of Renaissance architecture in England by nearly a hundred years, and left hideous scars on churches all over Europe. If we compare the plan of a pre-Reformation church with a post-Reformation one, the difference is obviously due to the changed nature of the service. In the latter, emphasis has shifted from the altar to the pulpit and with the removal of the chancel screen more 'congregation-participation' was possible. A visit to St. Stephen, the most delightful of Sir Christopher Wren's churches, in the City of London, shows how completely open the church became, and how the pagan classical forms were adapted for Christian worship. Other Wren churches, such as that of St. James, Piccadilly, show how the development of choral singing by the congregation and the growth of church organ music demanded the erection of galleries. Spires, always a prominent feature of church architecture, were now required to be placed on churches based on forms of classical temples, and Wren's genius is perhaps best shown by the richness and variety of his spires.

During this time, churches on the continent of Europe were emerging altogether unlike the restrained Wren churches. The Baroque was reaching its peak, particularly in Austria, early in the eighteenth century. The monastery at Melk, a Benedictine Abbey begun by Jakob Prandtauer in 1702, is far more an expression of an architectural theory than a building whose plan is determined by the demands of a religious order—it would have served equally well as a palace for a minor Danubian prince. The same criticism might almost be levelled

1

(1) The church of Val-de-Grâce, Paris, (1645–65). (2) A variety of spires showing the inventiveness of Sir Christopher Wren. (3) The Baroque Monastery at Melk, Austria, (1089; rebuilt 1702–49).

3

2

St. Martin-in-the-Fields,
London,
by James Gibbs, (1725).

St. Michaels, Charleston,
South Carolina.

at the Karlskirche, in Vienna, a superb example of the virtuosity of the Baroque craftsmen. In Spain, full rein was given to the ebullience of the Baroque in such features as the Transparente Chapel in the cathedral at Toledo. But here the Reformation gained no foothold and the architectural development was assisted rather than checked by the Counter-Reformation. In strong contrast is the severity of the small meeting houses of the new Non-Conformists and their counterparts in America. Charles Wesley had declared that the ideal plan for a church was octagonal, one in fact in which priesthood and congregation are one.

In England, the movement toward a restrained classicism in church architecture continued with such architects as Nicholas Hawksmoor, whose craggy Baroque is sometimes replaced by a strange 'Gothick' style, and the Roman-trained Scot, James Gibbs. Gibbs admitted his debt to Wren in his famous St. Martin-in-the-Fields. This church was more Wren-like and less Baroque than his St. Mary-le-Strand, an earlier church built after the Act of Parliament of 1711, to 'provide 50 new churches in or near the cities of London, and Westminster, or the Suburbs there of'.

Not only Gibbs' churches were influential but also his books, which enabled architects as far away as Boston to erect churches almost indistinguishable from those in Europe. Peter Harrison, an emigrant Yorkshireman, built the King's Chapel in Boston, a town which also possesses Christ Church, a copy of Wren's St. James's, Piccadilly. Meanwhile, copies of St. Martin-in-the-Fields, notably Christ Church, appeared in Philadelphia, and Gibbs' influence is apparent in the first Baptist Meeting House built in 1775 on Rhode Island by Joseph Brown. This timber building has a spire copied from that of St. Martin-in-the-Fields. English influences were not the only ones at work in American church architecture. Apart from his famous Capitol building, Benjamin Latrobe prepared several designs, including one Gothic project, for the cathedral at Baltimore, and the building which eventually emerged owed something to the Panthéon, in Paris.

Jacques Germain Soufflot's great domed church of St. Geneviève, called the Panthéon after the French Revolution, was an unusual design for France. It owed a good deal to St. Paul's

The Karlskirche, Vienna, by
Fischer von Erlach, (1715–37).

The stark interior of an early Non-Conformist meeting house in America.

St. Pancras Church, London— designed from details of classical Greek temples.

cathedral in London in the design of the dome on its colonnaded drum, placed over the crossing of the arms of what is almost a Greek cross. Built over a period of several years, from 1755–92, the Panthéon was to be described as 'between the massive architecture of Antiquity and the lighter Gothic architecture'. Soufflot used iron embedded in mortar to lighten the structure, made a new assessment of the then-despised Gothic architecture and personally investigated the classical temples at Paestum, drawing them in great detail in 1750.

With architects becoming interested in both Gothic and classical buildings the function of the church became of secondary importance; the emphasis was placed on the 'correctness' of detail. The plan of the building might remain the same, basically, so long as the appearance resembled that of a known classical building or was decked out in details recognizably derived from great European cathedrals. In London, in 1819, W. H. Inwood and his son started St. Pancras church, a magnification

All Saints, Margaret Street, London; a brick church of the Gothic Revival.

Interior of St. Jean de Montmartre, in reinforced concrete, (1894), by Anatole de Baudot.

of the tiny Erechtheum built in 420-393 B.C. Unfortunately the original lacked a spire and was also unaccountably non-symmetrical. Undeterred, the Inwoods concocted a 'classical' spire by piling classical elements one above the other, using a replica of the Athenian 'Tower of the Winds' as part of the structure. They copied the small caryatid porch to make twin cast-iron structures covered with terracotta forming a symmetrical plan. Auguste Pugin, a devout 'Gothic' architect, was as fervent in his denunciation of 'pagan' churches of this kind for Christian worship, as he was in his advocacy of the Gothic style. His own churches were wiry Victorian parodies of the splendor of the Middle Ages.

In France, Eugène Viollet-le-Duc, an architect and writer, thoroughly investigated the structural methods employed by the Gothic builders and, although some of his restorations have been severely criticized, swept away a good deal of romantic nonsense. In 1894 his disciple, Anatole de Baudot, designed

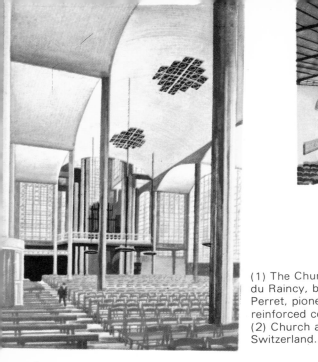

(1) The Church of Notre Dame
du Raincy, by the brothers
Perret, pioneers in the use of
reinforced concrete, (1922–23).
(2) Church at Zurich-Altstetten,
Switzerland.

St. Jean de Montmartre, the first church to be built in reinforced concrete, and in doing so he laid the foundations of
modern church architecture. But Baudot, while using a modern
material, still clung to the Gothic forms. For him, reinforced
concrete was still a synthetic stone, not a material in its own
right. It was left to his fellow countryman, Auguste Perret, to
develop a technique of concrete building suitable for church
architecture, some years later (1922-23).

Perret's Notre Dame, at Le Raincy, with its stress on the reinforced concrete structure and exposed materials, is oddly reminiscent of the wide areas of window and skeletal appearance of
English churches of the Perpendicular period. The church is
flooded with light; the bones beautiful. The plan is a simple
rectangle—not unlike that of an ancient basilica. Some four
years later, in 1927, Karl Moser designed his church of St.
Anthony, in Basle, in concrete, steel and glass.

In Germany serious consideration was being given not just to
the architectural idiom which should be used to build the
modern church but the very nature of worship in the twentieth

century itself. The church of Corpus Christi, built by Rudolf Schwarz in Aachen in 1930, revealed a deepening concern for re-assessing buildings for worship for the twentieth-century man. It is pared down to the barest essentials so that nothing shall distract the worshipper or the priest.

The political situation soon made it difficult for liberal architects to continue their work in Germany. The next important church was in Switzerland, again by Moser, at Zurich-Alstetten. The basic qualities for architectural integrity which modern architects were re-discovering and re-affirming all over Europe had been taken for granted by Moser. What he created in Zurich, according to Father A. H. Reinhold, was a new house for divine worship, not an autonomous architectural expression of religious feeling. Other architects, too, were concerned with a return to fundamental design for worship, instead of the re-creation of buildings which had served other communities worshipping in very different ways. A succession of churches following this thinking appeared, such as the circular church of St. Englebert, Riehl, built in 1928 by Dominikus Böhm, and his later cruciform church with a free-standing altar at Ringenberg.

A modern Dutch church at Leeuweriken Laan, Holland.

Notre-Dame du Haut, Ronchamp, France, by Le Corbusier,
(1950–54) is a pilgrimage church designed for 'outside' worship.

The desperate need for all kinds of churches in the cities of devastated Europe forced architects again to first principles. Le Corbusier re-built the bombed pilgrimage church of Notre-Dame at Ronchamp in an entirely different idiom. He deliberately created a romantically rough surface and provided a complex plan to accommodate altars for the direction of worship to the pilgrims in the open air.

In the New World, the Roman Catholic Church proved itself to be one of the most enterprising patrons of modern architects. Félix Candela, a refugee to Mexico from Spain, realizing that reinforced concrete construction had much in common with the traditional *adobe* technique of Mexico, designed some of the most exciting shell concrete churches in the world. Of these, perhaps the Church of the Miraculous Virgin will suffice to show his genius.

In Europe, it is not in the new cathedrals, such as that at

114

(1) Church of the Miraculous Virgin, by Félix Candela, Mexico, (1954). (2) Cathedral of Christ the King, Liverpool.

Coventry or Guildford, that we must look for a new approach to church architecture, but in a number of more humble parish churches all over Europe. In England, Bosanquet's little triangular-shaped church at Letchworth is one of the most inspiring of modern churches. The spire pierces the roof to act as a background to the free-standing altar, and to frame a fiberglas figure of the risen Christ to which all the aisles converge. The Reformed church just southwest of Haarlem in Holland built by Karel Sijmons shows very clearly the nature of the ritual for which it is designed, for here the congregation in turn actually sits at the table for eucharist. The breaking down of the barrier between priest and congregation, always a feature of the Non-Conformist worship, is being developed more and more by the other denominations, and the increasing number of church plans with such devices as the centralized altar is making this more than a theological hope. We are almost back to the early Christian church designs.

Buildings for Education

The requirements for education, until fairly modern times, were so simple that there was little need for specialized architecture, and existing buildings could be adapted without any difficulty. Almost any room would suffice which contained the pupils within reach of a strong right arm and in which they could read and write. During the Middle Ages education was entirely the affair of the Church, and education was carried out either on the premises of the monastery or abbey, or the three or four hundred grammar schools which existed by the fourteenth century and which were directly under the control of Church establishments. The main reason for their existence was the maintenance of a supply of literate clergy. It was for this purpose that William of Wykeham founded Winchester College and Henry VI founded Eton College, but such schools were also the only source of supply of clerks required for the efficient administration of the State. Inevitably the university buildings such as New College, Oxford, also founded by William of Wykeham, followed the architectural pattern of the monastery, with the main buildings grouped around a quadrangle, a fine chapel instead of the abbey church, refectory and lodgings for the scholars, and all the essential rooms grouped in a logical and beautiful pattern.

The Reformation, with its dissolution of the monasteries, greatly increased the need for grammar schools, but these, unlike the additions to the universities, followed the architectural pattern of domestic building, and their sixteenth-century remnants are still to be seen in some English towns today. It was from such a grammar school that a man as humbly born as William Shakespeare was to emerge.

Where existing church buildings could be used for educational purposes they were taken over, as at Leiden, Holland, for example, where the university (then an academy) confiscated the church of a convent built in 1516, a building it still occupies. In England, the college system, which replaced the

(1) Eton College, showing a monastic plan applied to a Tudor school. (2) St. John's College, Cambridge. (3) Winchester College, a medieval foundation.

1

2

3

(1) The formal façade of the Church of the Sorbonne, Paris. (2) The Sheldonian Theatre, Oxford, built by Sir Christopher Wren. (3) New College, Oxford, where medieval forms are revived in a Victorian setting.

hostelries and lodging houses of early medieval times, was a product of the Elizabethan period and was evolved for the better discipline and administration of Oxford and Cambridge.

The academic subjects taught both in schools and at university colleges required little modification to the established pattern of educational buildings for many hundreds of years, and any changes were due more to the dictates of fashion than to any academic demands. It was necessary, naturally, that university buildings should reflect current architectural trends, and their chapels assumed the appearance of new churches being designed all over Europe. Jacques Lemercier, the French architect who in 1635 built the new chapel for the Sorbonne in Paris, the most famous theological college in Europe, used the current Baroque style. Some years later, in about 1661, Le Vau built the great chapel which forms the centerpiece of the Collège des Quatre Nations in the same impressive manner as his work at Versailles. In England, Wren's additions to the university buildings of Oxford and Cambridge did little to disturb the existing medieval plans, however much they differed in style. His Sheldonian Theatre, designed for the recitation of prize compositions and the granting of honorary degrees is, however, in the contemporary style of the mid-seventeenth century. In the United States, in the eighteenth century, many of the college buildings reflected the austerity of the Puritans in examples of New England architecture.

Changes in school buildings were far less marked, but as new foundations were made they too were built in a somewhat humbler version of the contemporary style. The Dissenters, excluded from universities and from some schools by law, developed an excellent series of schools during the early eighteenth century and stimulated the established Church into producing a great many charity schools of their own. A much needed reform of the endowed schools took place during the next century, and the revived 'public schools' not only set their own houses in order, academically, but extended their buildings to accommodate the sons of the new aristocracy of the Industrial Revolution.

119

Many, with charters dating back to the Reformation, decided that their buildings should reflect their claims to antiquity by assuming a Gothic and semi-religious appearance. Schools and colleges with an emphatically ecclesiastic appearance and a monastic segregation, it was felt, were a suitable environment for the inculcation of a muscular Christianity and good learning. Architects such as Alfred Waterhouse and William Butterfield worked at Oxford and Cambridge and at public schools, and new schools and universities both in the United States and in England were quick to adopt the Gothic idiom for their new buildings.

After World War II, the urgent need for schools more capable of accommodating the more liberal and diverse forms of education created a remarkable renaissance of school building. It is true that magnificent school buildings of a specialized kind had appeared as early as 1919; the Bauhaus in Dessau had shown what a genius such as Gropius could produce in the way of educational buildings in 1925, and his village colleges in Cambridgeshire, built in collaboration with Maxwell Fry later, were to be landmarks in educational architecture; but the ordinary grammar schools built directly after the war were very different from anything that came before. At Hunstanton, in Norfolk, Alison and Peter Smithson were to exert a profound influence on school design by the production in 1954 of a building which was, in effect, a skin built around the complex activities of modern secondary education. Modern schools owe little to traditional school design and their freshness has impressed architects with the need to reassess the problems of building for education. The lightness and frank construction of modern grammar schools perhaps owe something to a superb educational building of this time, the Illinois Institute of Technology, built by Mies van der Rohe in Chicago. Here are shown great window areas and the honestly exposed constructional frame.

Like their contemporaries in other fields, university and school builders no longer find it necessary to hark back to the past but, having examined the entirely new concept of education, have realized that the methods of designing schools must be drastically revised. Facilities are now required

(1) The Illinois Institute of Technology, Chicago, a modern educational building by Mies van der Rohe, (1952–56). (2) A modern grammar school

1

2

which were undreamed of by the 'chalk and talk' methods of teaching in the past, and it is clear that buildings must not only provide these but be sufficiently flexible to be adapted to the changing needs of education. Since World War II, many of our colleges and universities have experienced overcrowded conditions because of an ever-increasing student body. To alleviate this problem a quick, efficient and inexpensive method of construction was utilized. Entire schools, as well as individual classrooms, have been rapidly assembled from specially designed mass-produced units made in factories. The basic structural members are of steel, with a wide variety of cladding, and the schools which have been constructed in this way have proved to be highly efficient, comparatively cheap and, in many cases, attractive. The New York State University system is expanding very rapidly and has made successful use of this system of construction. With the exception of the large

Modern buildings at the University of Mexico; on the far right is the library, its colorful mosaics blend modern architecture with traditional Mexican design.

The Freudenberg High School,
Zurich, Switzerland, a modern
school complex.

city areas where congestion is such that school buildings
tend to be large and impersonal, most modern schools are
spread out along just one story and contain informally ar-
ranged classrooms with movable furniture and effective
lighting.

UNESCO offers a service whereby the success of schools
such as the Freudenberg High School at Zurich, the
Bousfield Primary School in London, the School Center
at Madrid University or the buildings of Sussex University can be studied in relation to the problems of school
buildings in any part of the world, and modern techniques
of construction can be adapted for university or school
buildings in very different countries.

123

Buildings for Work

The transformation that such men as Matthew Boulton, Abraham Darby and Josiah Wedgwood effected during the mid-eighteenth century was to call for buildings without precedent in architecture. Wedgwood designed his own factories and, as he learned to organize his employees, ended by producing a well-designed and humane 'company town' which he called Etruria. His factory was organized around, as we would say today, his 'production flow'. This began at the canal bank where the raw materials were landed and moved from room to room; from the painting rooms to the kiln rooms, to the accounting room and finally to the stock rooms back on the canal bank, ready for transport. 'Useful wares' were separated from 'Ornamental wares', and his workmen were trained to be specialists in one aspect of the manufacture so that the factory grew quite naturally around the essential pattern of production.

Workers in other industries were less fortunate. The 'dark Satanic mills' of which poet William Blake wrote (himself an employee of Wedgwood) were producing conditions for the new conscripts of the industrial army as bad as those in the armed forces of that time. There were, of course, enlightened employers. Titus Salt, for example, the developer of alpaca, visited the Great Exhibition of 1851, hoping to buy the building afterward to make the lightest and most airy factory in England. But his advisers persuaded him it was not suitable and he built a company town called Saltaire instead, in 1852. The Cadbury family, the chocolate manufacturers, built their own garden city at Bournville in 1879, and experiments like these produced factories and environments far superior to any of the ordinary factory towns of northern England. Few people, however, considered that factory buildings could be anything other than squalid and ugly. Ebenezer Howard's vision of his first garden city, finally built at Letchworth from 1905 onward, not only included beautiful homes but beautiful factories too.

A typical factory scene in nineteenth-century England. Working conditions were still bad, but gradually improved after 1850.

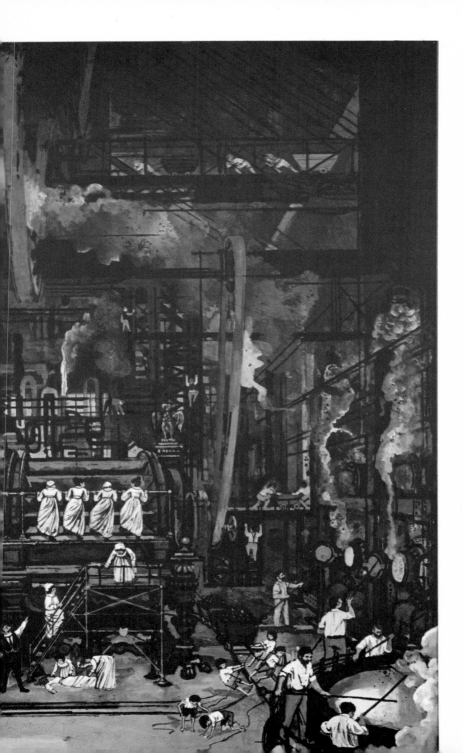

(1) Boots Chemical Factory, Beeston, Nottinghamshire, England (1930). (2) Shell Building, The Hague, Holland. (3) Van Nelle Tobacco Factory, Rotterdam, Holland; a new concept of industrial architecture.

1

2

3

In America and on the mainland of Europe, factory buildings were more readily accepted as legitimate architecture than in England, where a factory had to be camouflaged to look like something else. Thus, a factory chimney on the south bank of the Thames was so disguised that it used to look like a Venetian Gothic campanile on fire. In Germany, however, thanks largely to the Deutsche Werkbund, a number of architects were creating machine forms and industrial architecture of great distinction. One of the first was the A E G turbine factory built by Peter Behrens in Berlin in 1908, the first German building in glass and steel. Behrens' former pupils, Walter Gropius and Adolph Meyer, developed the new tradition by building the Fagus factory at Alfeld-an-der-Leine some three years later, and the very impressive model factory with its glass curtain walls at the Deutscher Werkbund exhibition at Cologne, just before World War I. During the recovery from war, other countries, notably Holland, continued to make their contribution to the development of industrial architecture. Johannes Brinkman and Mart Stam produced the Van Nelle Tobacco Factory in Rotterdam (1928–30) with reinforced concrete floors supported on mushroom-headed columns and with light screen walls, a device somewhat similar to that employed by E. Owen Williams at Beeston, near Nottingham, for the extension to the Boots Chemical Factory. The Shell Building in The Hague, built by Jacobus Oud in 1938, is a good example of the functionalist architecture being developed today in many parts of the United States and Europe.

The political regime that drove such distinguished architects as Ludwig Mies van der Rohe, Walter Gropius, Marcel Breuer and Erich Mendelsohn into exile was unwittingly to stimulate architectural thought in the United States, England and any country which offered them sanctuary. American architects derived enormous benefits from the presence of Mies van der Rohe at the Illinois Institute of Technology in Chicago and from Walter Gropius at the architectural school at Harvard. But in Europe, and especially in England, industrial architecture suffered a decline. This can be seen only too well by looking at the ribbon

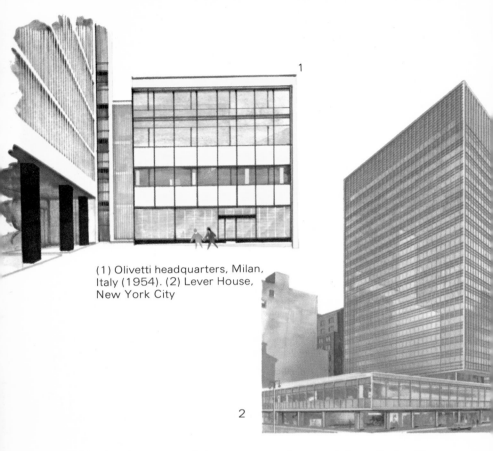

(1) Olivetti headquarters, Milan, Italy (1954). (2) Lever House, New York City

development of factories on the arterial roads leading out of London.

The vast rebuilding programs necessitated by the devastation of World War II produced some notable examples of every kind of architecture. Economy demanded that resources should be used to the utmost, and every advance in methods and materials enlisted in the rebuilding program.

In France, the devastated town of Royan had to be largely rebuilt, and one of the best of its many smaller buildings is the covered market. Its undulating roof, a concrete shell little more than three inches thick, is a brilliant example of economy of form and material. No less successful is the Exhibition Hall for the Centre National des Industries et des Techniques in

Paris, a huge vault built like the wing of an airplane with a prefabricated frame enclosed between two shells of concrete about five feet apart.

In South Wales, one of the most successful buildings, both economically and architecturally, is the rubber factory at Bryn Mawr built by Architects' Co-Partnership in conjunction with the engineer Ove Arup. The factory has a series of nine concrete bays lit with low domes with arc-shaped windows on four sides, a feature which is not only most efficient but extremely pleasant to look at from outside the building. Despite the dispersal of London's population to neighboring suburbs, great office blocks continue to rise in the center of London. One notable example is the 'Daily Mirror' building by the veteran architect, E. Owen Williams, who had pioneered the Boots building at Beeston in the 1930's and had produced the equally exciting 'Daily Express' building in 1931, with the first curtain wall to appear in London.

(1) The rubber factory at Bryn Mawr, Wales, built in conjunction with Ove Arup.

(2) Pellos Oy Chipboard Factory, Finland.

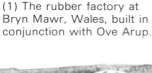

1

2

In Scandinavia, the cardboard factory at Fors, about 100 miles northwest of Stockholm, has to deal with enormous quantities of moisture extracted from the pulp in the course of manufacture, a forbidding task in a climate with its bitterly cold winters, and has to be very long to accommodate straight-line machinery. Ralph Erskine, the architect, considered both of these factors and solved the production problems with great ingenuity and beauty. There the basic building material is brick.

In Finland, there has been a tradition of fine industrial architecture for some time. The magnificent Sunila Sulphate-cellulose Plant built by Alvar Aalto at Kotka has been called the finest industrial complex in the world. On a smaller and lighter scale is the charming Knitted Goods Factory built by Viljo Revell at Hanko, a building far removed from the heavy brooding quality of much industrial architecture elsewhere. More recent is the huge chipboard and plywood factory at Pellos Oy, Ristiina, with accommodation for workers and essential buildings such as sauna baths as part of a beautifully landscaped complex. The chief architect is Korhonen, and most buildings are of the traditional white brick and timber.

In Italy, new materials have been used with considerable success by native architects. If Aalto is the genius of Finland, Pier Luigi Nervi may claim to be that of Italy. His first major post-war building was the superb Palazzo delle Esposizioni in Turin, a pre-fabricated reinforced concrete construction composed of small beautifully designed elements, referred to

Covered market at Pescia, Italy

Glass and steel International Arrival Building at Kennedy Airport, New York City (1962).

already in the chapter on reinforced concrete. Nervi was also one of the structural advisers to Gio Ponti and the team who built what must be one of the finest office blocks in Europe, the Pirelli building in Milan. This is a 33-story building, the construction of which depends on two central structures 416 feet high from which the floors are cantilevered to form, not a rectangular block, but a subtle angular-ovoid shape with glittering glass sides but almost solid ends. The offices of Alitalia, in Rome, have curtain walls of rigid foam-cored plastic which acts as more than a mere insulating screen.

In Pescia, the light and witty touch which one has come to associate with Italian architects is apparent in the seemingly weightless roof of the flower and vegetable market, which is secured by reinforced concrete buttresses and is made from

hollow tile arcs coated above and below to make them weather-proof.

In Switzerland, a superbly light building designed for the Aluminium Industries Headquarters by Hans Hofmann not only displays the effective combination of steel structure with different forms of aluminum, but also emphasizes the point that functional industrial architecture need not be dull or heavy.

The same lightness appeared in the United States as early as 1936–39, when Frank Lloyd Wright built the S. C. Johnson administrative building at Racine, Wisconsin, with an unprecedented fragility of construction. The main floor of the building is supported by a number of slender reinforced concrete mushrooms, formed by tapering pillars only nine inches in diameter at the base, but over 24 feet high, that bloom into discs 18 feet in diameter. The apparent fragility disturbed the authorities who loaded a test column with over 60 tons of gravel and cement and even then failed to smash it. Spaces between the concrete discs are filled with a ceiling of tubular glass.

This airy appearance is also to be found in Wright's Johnson Wax Tower, built in 1950. The floors of this structure are cantilevered out from a central concrete mast and have curtain walls of alternate bands of reddish brick and glass. This effect of lightness, which graces much of the more recent American architecture, may be traced back to the influence of Mies van der Rohe.

The same lightness and frank acceptance of structure is to be found in the General Motors Technical Center built at Warren, Michigan, by Eero Saarinen, the son of the Finnish architect, Eliel Saarinen, who built the railroad station at Helsinki at the beginning of the twentieth century. It is also to be seen in the work of Skidmore, Owings and Merrill, who built the Lever House in New York City (see page 128), one of the most sensitive architectural firms in the United States today.

For the first time, the architect can avail himself of a reflecting surface and a transparency that do much to mitigate the huge scale of some of the buildings of a modern industrial city.

Knitted goods factory, Hanko, Hopearanta, Finland. Interior of the Johnson Wax factory in Wisconsin, by Frank Lloyd Wright. Industrial complex at Lacq, France.

Prison Buildings

The cruelly efficient cellars in which prisoners were housed in the Middle Ages eventually came to be known by the word *donjon*, which originally meant the whole keep of a medieval castle. Most early city jails were part of the massive city gates, and a well-preserved example, the Gevangenpoort in The Hague, still survives. Such fortresses as the Tower of London were used for the imprisonment of important political prisoners.

Eighteenth-century prison at Old Newgate, London, now demolished.

Where buildings were specially designed as prisons, they take the appearance of contemporary domestic buildings, apart from the absence of windows and a more robust construction of the main door. The vivid pictures drawn by William Hogarth of the interior of Bridewell are sufficient for us to see how the interiors were organized. One of the most impressive was Newgate jail, built between 1770 and 1778 by George Dance the Younger. The central block in which the keeper lived had many windows, but the wings in which the prisoners were housed had none facing the outside, and the whole building was rusticated and grimly ponderous. A contemporary writer observed, 'The solid masses of its granite walls, strong enough to resist artillery, unbroken by door or casement — save those low and narrow slits in the center, iron-bound and mounted as they are—frown down upon the great arteries of London as the Bastille formerly did upon the Rue St. Antoine'. [Later prisons were designed with a central tower with radiating corridors of cells, and Holloway prison was described as 'a noble building of the castellated style', when it was first opened in 1852.]

With the development of an enlightened approach to the treatment of the criminal, more humane facilities are now being built within the prison to accommodate libraries, cafeterias, recreation rooms, work rooms and so on. The next few decades should see much innovation in prison construction in the United States.

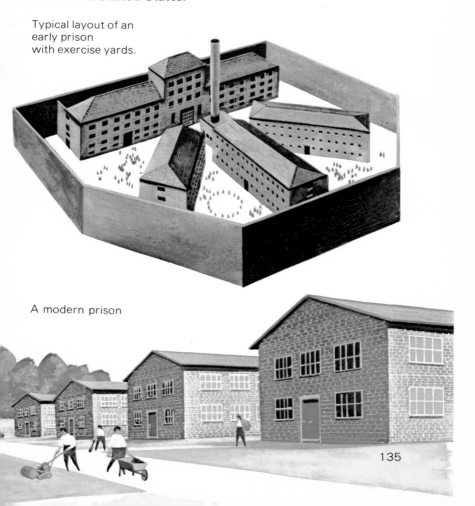

Typical layout of an early prison with exercise yards.

A modern prison

Hospital Buildings

During the Middle Ages, hospitals were the concern of the Church, who provided medical and nursing staffs as well as the buildings. Basically such buildings as the Hôpital St. Jean, in Bruges, or the hospital of St. Bartholomew, in London, were dormitories for nursing the ill and wounded. The Foundling Hospital in Florence, designed by Brunelleschi in about 1419, was an orphanage, whereas the hospital of St. Mary, in Chichester, which retains its medieval pattern, was, and still is, a home for old poeple. It is like a large church, with a chapel at the chancel end and little cubicles lining each side of the nave. The earliest isolation hospitals were for lepers and the mentally sick.

It was not until advances in medical science made it necessary to re-think the design of hospitals, that we get the groups of buildings of such complexity as those today. Bellevue Hospital Center in New York City covers over 20 acres, and some of its buildings are 22 stories high. It has been called 'a city within a city', an apt description when we consider some of the necessities of even a small modern hospital. One of the most famous of the specialized hospitals is that built by Alvar Aalto in Finland, from 1930 onward, at Paimio. Since World War II, a design which embodies everything learned about the needs of a modern hospital has been evolved at Saint-Lô, in Normandy, a complex 400-bed hospital designed by a team headed by Paul Nelson and, notable for its spheroid operating theaters. In the United States, many newer hospitals have been designed in such a way as to remove the vast, impersonal appearance so intimidating to many patients in larger buildings.

(1) A wing of Greenwich Hospital, England, by Sir Christopher Wren. (2) A sanatorium at Paimio, Finland, by Alvar Aalto, (1929–33). (3) An example of a modern clinic.

136

1

2

3

137

Roman Senate House from the Forum Romanum.

Rathaus at Bremen, Germany.

Opposite: Capitol building in Washington, D.C. was modeled after Christopher Wren's St. Paul's Cathedral in London.

Civic Buildings

When St. Paul declared himself 'a citizen of no mean city' his boast would have been echoed by inhabitants of any of the great cities of the Roman Empire, where the public buildings nourished a proper civic pride. During the Middle Ages, the Church was the supreme power, and her buildings, built to the glory of God, commanded the best brains, the best skills and the best materials for their construction and beautification. As secular power grew, some of these resources were diverted to other kinds of buildings, and in England the Reformation meant that all were used for the construction of the fine manor houses of the emergent ruling classes. In Italy, the rival city-states of Florence, Siena, Milan and others published their pride by the erection of magnificent town halls worthy of the city councils who ruled in them. In France, the *Hôtel de Ville,* or town hall, is different in style but no less beautiful than

138

corresponding buildings in Flanders, or the *Rathaus* of many German cities. The town hall in Italy is characterized by a mighty campanile, or bell tower, with a splendid council chamber as the core of the plan. The superb Piazza della Signoria in Florence is dominated by the Palazzo Vecchio and its towering bell tower. The Palazzo Pubblico in Siena is a similar civic building with a tower over 330 feet high. Both were built toward the end of the thirteenth century.

The hôtel de ville and the *palais de justice* of the French city came a little later, for their appearance depended on a degree of democracy not readily available under a feudal system. Those at Bourges and Dreux are detailed like a medieval church with crocketted ogee arches over the doors and windows and a general spikiness of roofline. The splendor of the town halls and guildhouses built by the burghers of the free cities in the Netherlands—Bruges, Ghent and Brussels—rivals that of the civic buildings of the city-states of Italy. The famous Belfry at Bruges, over 350 feet high, and the huge town hall at Brussels are typical of this remarkable manifesta-

An ostentatious 'hôtel de ville' in France.

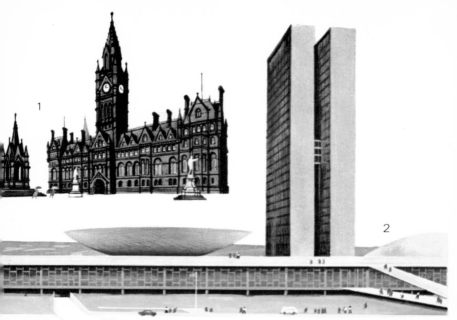

(1) Manchester Town Hall, England. (2) The Congress Building, Brasília, Brazil.
Opposite: United Nations Secretariat building, New York City, constructed in 1950. It was designed by several architects representing different countries.

tion of the civic pride which expressed itself in public buildings as well as in the smaller merchant houses which line the canals of the cities of Holland and Belgium.

Few buildings in the British Isles can compare with the civic buildings on the continent of Europe. Exceptions are the charming little Guildhall at Norwich, and the town hall at Windsor built by Sir Christopher Wren. But only in Dublin do we find a really magnificent range of civic buildings, including the Custom House, the Four Courts and additions to Parliament House, all built by James Gandon toward the end of the eighteenth century. Not until the nineteenth century did the city councils of the industrial towns of northern England, which had grown with incredible rapidity, decide to enhance their prestige by the erection of huge municipal buildings.

In America, too, a growing sense of identity began to express itself in civic buildings. One of the first American-born architects, President Thomas Jefferson, designed the

Virginia State Capitol at Richmond, Virginia, in the 1790's, somewhat in the classical style. The Capitol, in Washington, D.C. was designed by a West Indian doctor named William Thornton, and it provided a pattern for other state capitols.

Public buildings continued to be dressed either in a somewhat ostentatious 'Gothic' manner or in the more reticent domed classical style until fairly recent times. The example set by the Town Hall in Stockholm, built in a severe brick idiom, showed little sympathy with either historical style and displayed an originality on the part of the architect, Professor Ragnar Ostberg, which is refreshing without being brash. Mention should be made of the United Nations Building in Paris, a vast building designed by a committee of good architects, but one which shows this corporate effort too clearly; of the more recent daring experiment of Brasília, where buildings of great freshness and beauty are rising; and of the new capital of the Punjab, Chandigarh, where Le Corbusier worked with two English architects, Maxwell Fry and Jane Drew, to produce the first modern capital city in the Indian sub-continent.

The Law Courts, Brussels,
Belgium, by Joseph Polaert,
(1866–1883).

143

An early Victorian 'chain' pier at Brighton, (1823).

Buildings for Travel and Transport

Oddly enough travel by sea has not modified buildings very much. One of the most charming Customs Houses in Britain, that built at King's Lynn in 1683 by Henry Bell, with its well-proportioned square shape, steep roof and balustrade, is derived from the Royal Exchange, now destroyed, and from other buildings in Holland which have no particular connection with travel. There is a most elegant Customs House with a fine double staircase at Poole in Dorset, built in the eighteenth century, and heavily designed bonded warehouses of stone of about the same period still survive in Plymouth. Some of the finest early industrial architecture is still to be seen at St. Katherine's Dock, in London, and a vast complex has been designed at Tilbury to handle passengers and freight, with hotels and restaurants, administrative buildings and piers. A more impressively designed complex, however, can be seen from the top of the Euromast, in Rotterdam. The individual buildings may be considered somewhat unimaginative, but the overall effect is magnificent and the road pattern admirable.

During the ages, travel by road has had little direct effect on architecture, except to modify the shape of the coaching

inn so that the coaches could be driven right into the courtyard and the passengers alight in the shelter of the surrounding
balconies. Some of the original tollhouses still survive and can
usually be detected by their shape, which is often octagonal, or
by their positioning opposite each other to form the attachment
of the tollgate. More recently, the great arterial roads—the
freeway in the United States, the *Autobahn* in Germany, the
autostrada in Italy—have demanded their own form of architecture: filling stations, hotels and restaurants. Many of these
facilities, particularly in Italy, are well designed and do little
harm to the landscape.

It is a different matter when we turn from road to rail
transport. Once architects realized that they were confronted
with the problems of buildings for which there was no precedent, some very fine architecture was to appear. When railroads
were first introduced, they attracted such a storm of abuse
from writers such as William Wordsworth and John Ruskin,

A tollhouse with tollgate, showing coach arriving.

that their designers were obliged to find some way of making their buildings more acceptable. When we admonish the Victorians for concealing their stations behind Gothic or classical façades, we forget that these buildings were without precedent and that their designers had not been subjected to the conditioning by which we accept a brutal frankness of construction today without a qualm. The picturesque disguises adopted by the designers of railroads were condemned by Ruskin, who declared 'Railroad architecture has or would have a dignity of its own if only left to its work', a statement justified by the successful design of King's Cross Station in London. Its architect, Lewis Cubitt, paid little attention to historical decoration and concentrated on the provision of platforms, vestibules and other essential facilities.

An element of prestige also determined the appearance of certain railroad stations, particularly those in Paris, such as the Gare St. Lazare, and in Berlin. With the unification of Italy, stations in Turin, Milan, Naples and Rome all pay tribute to a great historical past. The huge nineteenth-century stations of America, now demolished, solved their functional problems admirably, but they were equally obsessed with prestige.

The Central Station at Helsinki, built just before World War I by Eliel Saarinen, was to prove an inspiration to later designers, and by the 1930's such stations as the Gare de Ville at Le Havre, show how the idea of 'a station which *is* a station' had evolved. In England, at about the same time, talented architects had been at work on different station problems, for the London Underground obviously had different needs from those of a great terminal station. The Underground stations at Arnos Grove, Cockfosters and Osterley Park have dated surprisingly little, and in Holland, the stations at Amsterdam (Amstel) and at Muiderpoort, both constructed in 1939, look more recent than their age. Since World War II, much rebuilding has been needed for railroad architecture. The new station at Harlow, England, harks back to the brutalism of the

(1) King's Cross Station, London, by Lewis Cubitt, (1851–52).
(2) Helsinki Station, Finland, by Eliel Saarinen, (1910–14).
(3) The interior of Arnos Grove Underground Station, London.
(4) Termini Station, Rome, showing the cantilever roof.

1

2

3

4

immediate post-war years, and the second Stazione Termini in Rome is an outstanding example of functional beauty.

Apart from an eccentric Tudor-style aircraft hangar built in the 1930's, airports have never been ruined by historical allusions, but have been based on the purely functional aspect of architectural design. Buildings have been planned solely for the services of the great machines and the passengers and freight they carry.

In the United States, the enormous distances which people travel forced their architects to regard the design of airports as a more urgent problem. Few airports in the world can boast of such large or beautiful buildings as the John F. Kennedy International Airport in New York City. Designed by architect Saarinen and constructed from reinforced concrete, the forms of the TWA building somehow make an allusion to those one finds in the aircraft themselves—sweeping curves with clean sharp contours and a sculptural quality. The only building perhaps of comparable quality is also in the United States, and is constructed, like the building at John F.

Buildings at Gatwick—
a great modern airport.
Interior of the airport
reception building,
St. Louis, Missouri

148

Sweeping concrete forms like the TWA building at John F.
Kennedy International Airport, New York City (1956–61)—airport
buildings for a jet age.

Kennedy Airport, from a series of concrete shell structures.
This is the airport reception building designed by George
Hellmuth, Joseph Leinweber and M. Yamasaki in St. Louis,
Missouri. It has great wings sweeping upward and freeing
whole areas of wall and ceiling for glazing. In many ways, the
designers of buildings for transport by air have avoided the
mistakes made by early railroad architects, and the resultant
buildings have a clarity of purpose and construction which
makes them some of the most characteristically beautiful of
this century.

The British realized only during the past few years what a
damaging impression their airports gave their country and
began to do something about it. One of the most successful of
the new airports is that at Gatwick, where a well-integrated
series of air, rail and road transport buildings have been
designed by the Yorke, Rosenberg and Mardall team. More
recently, Sir Basil Spence designed an airport at Glasgow
which is a marked advance on some earlier buildings.

Reconstruction of the Roman
Theater at Ostia, Italy.

The Globe Theater, a building
in Shakespearean England.

Buildings for Entertainment

Modern tourists are always surprised at the audibility of actors
performing on the open-air stages of Greece and Rome, but it
is clear, from the fifth book of Vitruvius, written in the first
century B.C., that the science of acoustics had been very
thoroughly investigated.

During the Middle Ages, traveling professional players set
up temporary booths or gave their performances in the courtyard of an inn such as 'The George' at Southwark, London,
and the pattern of the court with surrounding galleries
influenced the design of such theaters as the 'Globe' in which
Shakespeare performed. A detailed contract of construction
drawn up in 1600 for the 'Fortune' theater, which was closely
modeled upon that of the 'Globe', gives an accurate description of the three-story background with gallery and dressing

rooms for the accommodation of the players, and the arrangements for seating the audience.

Meanwhile, in 1580, Andrea Palladio, using Vitruvius' text, constructed the Teatro Olimpico at Vicenza, Italy. His design was based somewhat inaccurately on a classical theater with a stage platform backed by three-dimensional scenery with faked perspective producing an illusion of depth. This was, however, something of a freak, and in Florence the theater was assuming the familiar appearance of a rectangular hall, with proscenium arch, curtain and scenery. In England, the invention of removable scenery was put into practice by Inigo Jones for the masques at the court of James I and Charles I. The pattern of the eighteenth-century theater with horseshoe-shaped galleries around three sides of a rectangular room and the stage sealing off the end wall, established the design of the theater until fairly recent times, when a different concept of drama demanded a different kind of arrangement.

Plan of the Palladian Theater, Vicenza, Italy, showing falsified perspective of the scenery.
The eighteenth-century facade of Drury Lane Theater, London.

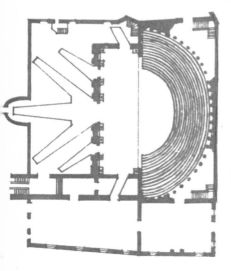

City Theater, Malmö, Sweden, with movable walls for reducing seating area.

A visit to the theater is a social occasion, and especially in the eighteenth and nineteenth centuries it was as important to be able to see who was in the audience as to see who was on the stage. A private box might give its occupants an oddly distorted view of the actors, but it gave them an excellent vantage point from which to study other members of the audience and conferred social prestige on those who were seen in it. Foyers, too, had to be large, impressive and richly embellished, and staircases had to be capable of allowing a procession of glittering personages to parade. The Opera House in Paris, built in 1874 by Charles Garnier represents the peak of this truly theatrical architecture, with its imposing *Escalier d'Honneur* and its great portico, encrusted with every kind of ornamental cliché.

The development of the technical devices which serve drama has also changed the appearance of theaters. Stages are sometimes so large that there is as much area behind the proscenium arch as in front. Recently, playwrights and pro-

Theater at Helsinki by Aalto

One building in Lincoln Center, New York City. Complex houses
an opera house, a museum, a music school, a symphony
hall and two theaters. These buildings were all designed
by different architects.

ducers have tried to involve their audiences by projecting the
forestage into the auditorium, and this 'theater in the round'
approach has considerably modified the design of new theaters. The abolition of the proscenium arch that this type of
theatrical production requires has meant that architects have
had to design theaters that are much more flexible in plan.
One outstanding example is the city theater at Malmö, in
Sweden, with an auditorium which, normally seating 1,200
people, has movable walls which can be used to reduce the
area for the production of more intimate plays. Even greater
flexibility of both auditorium and stage arrangements is to
be found in the Ebertplatz theater at Gélsenkirchen, where the
entrance lobby envelops the U-shaped auditorium on three
sides and insulates it from interference by noise.

Buildings for Sport

That the modern sports stadium differs so much from its counterpart in ancient Rome is not because its basic function is very different but because modern constructional techniques are able to give far better protection to the spectators than the classical *velarium*. This has been replaced by thin reinforced concrete shell forms which are cantilevered out and appear almost to float over the rings of seats, needing no columns or supports which would obscure the view. Certain kinds of sport can now be seen entirely under cover, and the beautiful reinforced concrete domes, such as that which roofs the Palazzo dello Sport, and its smaller partner, the Palazzetto dello Sport, both designed for the Olympic Games in Rome in 1960, are typical of the most modern constructional techniques for sports stadia. Less familiar perhaps are the methods employed by Eero Saarinen for the Yale Hockey Rink at Yale University, New Haven, Connecticut and used for a similar building on a much greater scale in Japan. Briefly, the construction of the Yale building consists of a sweeping concrete spine like the vertebrae of an animal supported at about the areas in which one would find the shoulder girdle and the pelvis of a prehistoric animal, with the tail and long neck extended. From this spine spreads a taut skin of roof, braced in position with guide wires, like a tent.

A more complex structure, but using the same constructional ideas, was built in Japan for the National Gymnasium in Tokyo and used for some events in the Olympic Games of 1964. Cables suspended between two huge pillars, much as in a suspension bridge, form the principal axes of the main gymnasium. At each end the backstays are secured to ensure stability. On either side are half-moon-shaped stands for spectators, which also supply vast structural arches, and the roof is suspended between the upper edges of these stands and the main axial cable. The whole structure is as tense as a tent, and great care had to be taken to ensure that the tensions were all correctly maintained. The architect, Kenzo Tange, saw this building not merely as an exercise in hydrodynamics. He also wanted to eliminate the oppressive feeling of a roof above and the sense of being enclosed caused by the flanking stands.

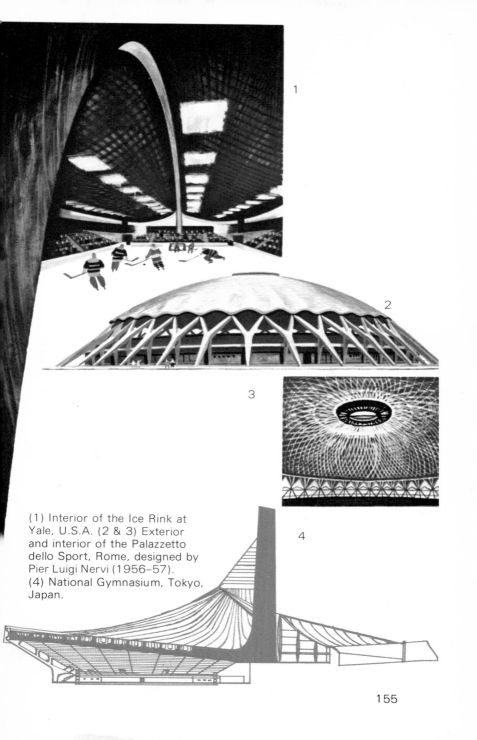

(1) Interior of the Ice Rink at
Yale, U.S.A. (2 & 3) Exterior
and interior of the Palazzetto
dello Sport, Rome, designed by
Pier Luigi Nervi (1956–57).
(4) National Gymnasium, Tokyo,
Japan.

BOOKS TO READ

Graphic History of Architecture. John Mansbridge. Viking, 1967.

Living Architecture series. (9 vols.) Grosset & Dunlap.

Architectural Principles in the Age of Humanism. R. Wittkower. Random House.

Early American Architecture. H. Morrison. Oxford University Press.

Mechanization Takes Command. S. Giedion. Oxford University Press, 1969.

Space, Time, and Architecture. S. Giedion. Harvard University Press, 1967.

The Architecture of Ancient Greece. W. B. Dinsmoor. Argonaut.

Architecture: The indispensable art. W. R. Dalzell. London: Michael Joseph, 1962.

Architecture: A Short History. J. Watterson. Norton.

Architecture in America. W. Andrews. Atheneum.

Architecture in America: A Battle of Styles. W. A. Coles and H. H. Reed, Jr. (eds.) Appleton.

Architecture in Transition. C. Doxiadis. Oxford University Press.

Architecture Today and Tomorrow. C. Jones. Mcgraw-Hill.

Architecture through the Ages. T. Hamlin. Putnam.

Modulor. Le Corbusier. Faber, 1954.

Le Corbusier. Peter Blake. Pelican, 1963.

Mies van der Rohe. Peter Blake. Pelican, 1963.

Looking and Seeing. K. Rowland. Volumes I–IV. Ginn, 1964.

The Cathedral Builders. Jean Gimpel. Oxford University Press, 1961.

An Outline of European Architecture. N. Pevsner. Pelican, 1960.

Pioneers of Modern Design. N. Pevsner. Pelican, 1960.

The Penguin Dictionary of Architecture. J. Fleming, H. Honour, and N. Pevsner, 1966.

An Introduction to Modern Architecture. J. M. Richards. Penguin, 1967.

INDEX

OTHER TITLES IN THE SERIES

The GROSSET ALL-COLOR GUIDES provide a library of authoritative information for readers of all ages. Each comprehensive text with its specially designed illustrations yields a unique insight into a particular area of man's interests and culture.

NOW AVAILABLE

SOON TO BE PUBLISHED